Praise for
101 Marketing Strategies

Not only is the book well-written and helpful to me, but I will ask all the attorneys in my firm to read 101 Marketing Strategies.

William H. Lassiter, Esq., Managing Partner
Lassiter, Tidwell & Hildebrand, PLLC
Nashville, TN

In a marketplace full of books that take professional services marketing to the level of rocket science, Troy Waugh strips out the rhetoric and delivers the professional services guide to common sense marketing. Taking all the experience that he has gathered over 30 years, Troy delivers a great collection of tips and ideas that can help any professional services firm jump-start their marketing efforts. Every professional should read this book.

Gordon Lee, National Director of Marketing
BDO Dunwoody LLP
Toronto, ON, Canada

Troy Waugh's latest book, 101 Marketing Strategies, is a must read in today's competitive world of selling professional services. Full of practical, results-based micro-actions, 101 Marketing Strategies is not about gimmicks, but about the proven effectiveness of building relationships and the discipline of process.

Bill Fingland, Managing Partner
BKD, LLP
Springfield, MO

Too often lawyers are too busy practicing law to pay enough attention to the business side of their practice. That's why 101 Marketing Strategies should be required reading for all legal professionals, from sole practitioners to managing partners of major law firms. Troy Waugh's practical, no-nonsense approach to setting business goals, building up and maintaining a lucrative client base, keeping employees happy and outselling the competition really works!

By implementing the marketing recommendations in this book, I have seen palpable improvements in my civil litigation practice. Having worked with Troy Waugh for years, I know that his blueprint for marketing is based on his many client successes. This is a book to be taken to heart by all professionals who are serious about building and expanding their businesses.

Robert L. Esensten, Esq.
Beverly Hills, CA

101 Marketing Strategies

for

Accounting, Law, Consulting, and Professional Services Firms

Troy Waugh

WILEY

John Wiley & Sons, Inc.

This book is printed on acid-free paper. ⊗

Library of Congress Cataloging-in-Publication Data:

Waugh, Troy.
   101 marketing strategies for accounting, law, consulting, and professional services firms / Troy Waugh.
      p. cm.
   Includes index.
   ISBN 0-471-65110-9
   1. Marketing—Decision making. 2. Strategic planning. 3. Customer relations—Management.   I. Title: One hundred one marketing strategies for accounting, law, consulting, and professional services firms.   II. Title.
   HF5415.135 .W38 2004
   658.8'02—dc22

                                                                    2003021210

Printed in the United States of America

10 9 8 7 6 5 4 3 2 1

About the Author

Troy Waugh, CPA, MBA, is a leading author, speaker, teacher, and consultant to the accounting industry. Troy helps public accounting firms grow. He and his experienced team of consultants have helped firms add more than $500 million in new business through their consulting, training, and alliance services.

Troy's highly acclaimed book *Power Up Your Profits,* has received praise throughout the world. It has been published in German and will soon be available in Japanese. Troy's articles have been published in *Accounting Today, The Practical Accountant,* and numerous state society monthly newsletters. He has been publishing *A Marketing Moment with Troy Waugh* since 1992. He is one of the most sought after speakers on sales and marketing professional services in the United States.

Troy is the founder of The Rainmaker Academy, the leading sales and marketing training course in the United States and Western Europe. The Rainmaker Academy is a three-year intensive sales training program whose graduates have attracted over $300 million to their firms during the classes.

He received an MBA in marketing from the University of Southern California and a BS in accounting from the University of Tennessee.

Troy was an audit manager with PriceWaterhouse & Co., where he worked six years in their Nashville and Los Angeles offices. During his years with PriceWaterhouse, Troy was active in the Los Angeles Junior Chamber of Commerce and many other activities.

In 1975, Troy became Chairman and Chief Executive Officer of Advantage Companies, Inc. During his eight years with Advantage, Troy guided a complete repositioning of the company's focus away from the budget motel business into magazine publishing. During this period, Troy negotiated over 40 acquisitions or divestitures of businesses.

In 1984, Troy became a Vice President with Jacques Miller, Inc., a real estate investment firm. He was promoted to Senior Vice President and National Sales Manager during his years with Jacques Miller, Inc. Due to theTax Reform Act of 1986, Troy was instrumental in repositioning the company away from tax-advantaged real estate in 1987 into high yielding health-care real estate and again in 1989 into real estate management.

He is a member of The Advisory Board, a national consortium of leading consultants to the professions, the National Speakers Association, The American Institute of CPAs, and The Tennessee Society of CPAs.

Troy Waugh may be reached at:

The Rainmaker Academy
4731 Trousdale, Suite 12
Nashville, TN 37221
phone: (615) 373-9880
email: *troy@waughco.com*

Our Team

Charles Flood

A professionally trained educator and businessman, Charlie has been on the front lines in sales, general management, and professional consulting for the past 20 years. His experience comes from work with national and local accounting firms, and in national sales management with a Fortune 500 company.

His academic credentials include a BA in education, BS in sociology, and a MEd with an emphasis on Educational Leadership Development. In addition, Charlie is certified to facilitate a number of professional development courses. Charlie's background, experience, and perspective bring an added dimension to the Rainmaker team of professionals.

Graham G. Wilson

Graham G. Wilson believes in the power of marketing and sales in public accounting. He joined The Rainmaker Academy in 1996. Over the past 20 years, he has combined extensive international content knowledge with outstanding facilitation skills to enable CPA firms, departments, and individuals to increase their marketing and sales effectiveness.

As a former client partner with Franklin Covey and as Director of Training for the largest local accounting firm in Chicago, Graham has unique insight into the development needs of accountants. Graham is a frequent speaker and program presenter for the Illinois CPA Society, and for many national and international accounting firms.

Graham holds both bachelor's and master's degrees from Southampton University, UK. Born in England, Graham moved to the United States in 1993 and became a U.S. citizen in 1997.

Patrick Patterson

Patrick is a professional trainer and facilitator with more than 10 years of experience in people and process development. Participants consistently rate energy, enthusiasm, skill, and insight as hallmarks of his presentations. He brings expertise in the area of quality and continuous improvement.

Patrick's background includes eight years in Continuous Improvement at Arizona State University and three years as a training and development consultant for Las Vegas, Nevada, resorts. He holds a bachelor's degree in communications from Brigham Young University. Patrick is a past Director of Professional Development (Las Vegas/Tucson Chapters), American Society for Training and Development.

Kevin Poppen

Kevin is Chief Operating Officer of the Enterprise Network and is responsible for the day-to-day operations. Kevin serves as the primary contact for the members, challenges them to think about their future, and helps them adopt strategies that will enhance their profits, owner value, and professional satisfaction.

Kevin comes to Enterprise Network from the RSM McGladrey Network, where he spent over seven years serving their membership. He filled a variety of roles, including member service, recruitment, and training on McGladrey & Pullen's audit and accounting guidance materials.

Before joining the McGladrey Network Office in July 1995, Kevin served on the audit and accounting team in McGladrey & Pullen's Moline, Illinois, office.

Scott Bradbary

Scott joined Waugh & Co in January 2003 as Director of Training for The Rainmaker Academy. He is a professional educator and curriculum specialist who will be working on the continued professionalism of the Rainmaker training materials. His background and research into learning styles, multimedia instruction, organizational health, and sense of community is a valuable addition to the Waugh & CO team.

Scott was a public school teacher for seven years before returning to graduate school at Vanderbilt. He is currently completing his doctoral requirements at Peabody College of Vanderbilt University in curriculum and instructional leadership. He served as an instructor at Vanderbilt in the College of Education at the undergraduate and graduate levels. He is a certified national training in the Classroom Organization and Management Program (COMP) and has conducted workshops across the southeast.

Scott holds an MEd in social science education from University of Georgia and a BA in history from LaGrange College.

Drew Crowder

A professional marketer and consultant, Drew joined Waugh & Co in 2000 and brings to the team a diverse skill set acquired through his marketing background in public relations, state politics, clinical software, and independent consulting.

Vice President of Consulting with Waugh & Co and a Nashville native, Drew has a BS in business administration and an MBA with a concentration in marketing.

The Rainmaker Academy

Our Mission

The mission of The Rainmaker Academy is to transform the lives of certified public accountants. We help our clients realize their lifestyle and profit potential through more effective communications.

Our Values

- To provide unsurpassed content excellence, marketing motivation, and value
- To promote a climate of trust, innovation, enthusiasm, teamwork and open dialog among our clients and associates
- To conduct our business with the highest standards of integrity consistent with our Christian values
- To seek to understand the critical needs of our clients and associates and to help create a sense of partnership among all

Our Commitment

All our work is fully guaranteed. If we fall short of your expectations, in any way, please contact us immediately so we can work to assure your happiness. Or, simply pay an amount you believe represents the value you received from us.

Contents

Preface

Most sales and marketing consultants subscribe to an "event" model of selling. You will find books written on single subjects such as closing the sale, referral selling, and overcoming objections. Many of these models and books are loaded against long-term success in selling professional services. Selling professional services is not an event, it is a process. Although pieces do have usefulness when placed in the context of the selling process, you may develop great skill in closing the sale and still not close many sales because you closed too soon or too late.

This book, addressed to senior associates and partners of accounting, law, consulting, and other professional business services, describes selling as a process. I cover the three levels of the selling process: (1) The development of the relationship, (2) the buying process of the client, and (3) the selling process of the professional. This is the process we use in The Rainmaker Academy, a leadership and business development program for professionals. It has been tested and found highly effective in hundreds of the world's most successful firms.

101 Marketing Strategies for Accounting, Law, Consulting, and Professional Services Firms has been over 30 years in its development. Beginning at PricewaterhouseCoopers in the late 1960s, I was more fascinated with practice development than the debits and credits. After obtaining my MBA from the University of Southern California in 1973, I knew that selling was in my future. But at that time, selling was *verboten* in the professions. What I did learn, as practice development leader in my office, was that the best sellers used a process. The best practice developers in the 1970s used processes that helped them avoid illegal and unethical sales tactics. In most cases, the processes relied on building relationships to a point where the prospects would ask the professional to serve them.

Let me describe one of those processes. Robert E. Healy was a partner in the New York office of Price Waterhouse & Co. (PW) in 1970. He was active in the accounting professional associations and head of the firm's Mergers and Acquisitions Department (M&A). As head of M&A, Bob Healy developed a national database of businesses, by industry code. Healy traveled the country meeting with CEOs of PW clients, discussing their interests in acquiring, divesting, or merging their businesses. In 1971, Healy, along with George D. McCarthy, wrote a book titled *Valuing a Company, Practices and Procedures.* He became a nationally recognized expert in the M&A business.

The clients that Healy would meet with would invariably ask him to contact other companies (many nonclients) in pursuit of M&A opportunities. Healy learned that as he built relationships with the nonclients over the M&A activity, the clients would share their dissatisfaction with the present accounting or tax services. Prospects sharing their dissatisfaction provided an ethical opening that Bob learned to develop into an urgency to change. I met Bob in 1974, when the firm asked him to open a practice office from scratch in Memphis. Within a few years the Memphis office became a thriving multimillion dollar practice office for PW. He built the Memphis office using the same process he'd used nationally. He could find a way to meet any CEO of any significant company in the market by opening the conversation with his national M&A expertise.

Bob Healy developed a process that some people call a sales funnel or pipeline. But, his process was legal and ethical. (The only things illegal and unethical were the sales and marketing events: advertising and solicitation.) And today, even though advertising and solicitation is legal and ethical, by themselves they aren't very effective.

After my experiences at PW, I enjoyed 16 years in pure sales and marketing roles in magazine publishing and investment real estate. In the intervening years, the business world became much more complex and fast paced, but in every case where I have experienced great success in selling, we have developed a process to fill the pipeline full of prospects and clients, all in different states of maturation. The people and firms who view selling as an event are the ones you meet who say, "We tried advertising once and it didn't work" or "We tried a seminar and only a few people came, so we gave up."

In 1991, I started my sales and marketing training and consulting business teaching a basic sales pipeline process from prospecting to building client loyalty. But in 1991 I seriously underestimated the degree to which "event marketing" was ingrained in the professions. After achieving only limited success for a few years, I began to experiment and build a teaching process that helped change the belief system and helped professionals develop their own unique selling processes.

One sales trainer told me that he felt very good after years of training professionals to sell despite the fact that he knew that almost no new business had developed as a result of his classes. This respected trainer maintained that his training was valuable because the professionals had learned about marketing and selling. In my view, mere insights and education into selling are of no value to professionals. I would feel my consulting was a dismal failure if the professionals did not increase sales success and attract more business.

Success in selling is a bit like swimming across a raging river. While your goal is get to the other side, the strong current of the river will have a lot to do with your eventual success. If you work with the river's currents, cross currents, twists, and turns, your odds of traversing the river are greatly improved. Fight the river and you will lose.

In successful selling there are two very powerful currents working: relationship development and the buying process. As described in this book, the relationship begins with discovery. As you meet people and learn about their businesses, you are sizing each other up in a variety of ways. If you use selling techniques that are effective in the decision phase of the relationship, when you are in the discovery phase, you will rarely succeed. You will be known as pushy, arrogant, and only self-interested. As the relationship building process moves into the differentiation phase, you and your prospect begin to sort through the myriad factors that ultimately determine a good fit. Factors such as size, scope, specialties, industry or services expertise, needs, wants, willingness and ability to pay fees, and time of year are just a few that you and your prospect must sort through. Once through the differentiation phase, you and your prospect enter the decision phase of the relationship. Assuming the decision is one to hire you, the final phase of the relationship is delivery.

In each phase of relationship development, the buyer proceeds through a well-documented and researched process of buying. In the discovery phase, the buyer prospect is becoming aware of you and developing an understanding of you and your firm. If you try to move to another phase too early, you will be fighting strong currents of opposition. During the differentiation phase, the prospect begins evaluating alternatives, recognizing needs and wants, and growing positive perceptions and attitudes about you and your firm. During the decision phase, the buyer is understanding the depth and breadth of your capabilities, handling his own indecisiveness, evaluating risk, and getting to an often painful decision to make a change. During the delivery phase, both you and the client are working to deepen the relationship to that of repeat customer or business partner.

Of course, if the buyer is in the decision portion of the relationship and is ready to buy, you do not want to step back to the discovery phase and waste a lot of time.

Because my goal is to build professionals who can sell, rather than sellers who happen to sell law or accounting services, I began writing a newsletter a few years ago. Well over 50 state and national associations and societies have published articles from the newsletter, titled *A Marketing Moment,* for their members. I have followed the pattern of the newsletter in this book. Short, pointed articles, mostly taken from my successful experience with selling situations, seem to help professionals grasp the essence of the topic. I have arranged these "strategies" in a format that will enable you to judge where you are in the cross-currents of relationship development and the buying process.

When you build a home, you don't begin with the roof. You begin with a drawing called a blueprint. In fact, you build the home on paper before you begin construction. Then during construction, if you follow your blueprint and plans, you won't start painting before you have all the trim work complete. The same is true with this blueprint. First find out where you are in the relationship-building process and learn where the buyer is before you implement your selling tactics. By using this blueprint, you can be much more successful.

In writing such a book, it has been necessary to make some broad generalizations. Many successful people have dealt with the issues raised in this book. The best way to deal with the generalities is to ask yourself, "Does this apply to me?" You can use your own experiences to decide what you must do to create more success in your selling.

Each chapter has several short strategies that are designed to help you be successful in that phase. There may be many cases when you feel you need more depth in a certain phase of selling. In that situation, please refer to the Reference Guide. The Reference Guide contains the best books, of which I am aware, that will help you with more in-depth knowledge of that subject.

Who Should Read this Book and Why

Owners and associates of accounting, law, consulting, and business services firms should read this book as a foundational tool. The professional who can also sell is a powerful force in the business world. This book is also addressed to marketing and sales directors and coordinators and consultants who work with professional firms. This book will be of particular interest to those who are specialists in event selling, such as brochure development, prospecting, closing, or client service. This will help each person to venture into all aspects of the selling process and to work within the currents of relationship and buyer development. This book is especially valuable to those charged with leading the professional firm: the managing partner, the chief operating officer, the chief marketing officer, the firm administrator, and the human resources director.

The professional who can sell is the master of his or her destiny. The professional who cannot sell becomes the victim of the system. If you cannot sell, you are prone to take only the work assigned to you or the prospects who call you because no one else wanted them. The book's goal is to help you build your personal and firm business more successfully. I want you to be able to measure your success, not by how much you *know* about selling, but by the results you get through what you *do* about selling.

I hope this book helps you to grow your practice.

Troy Waugh
Nashville, Tennessee
March 2004

Introduction

1 **Why Market?**

Everywhere I go, professionals ask, " Why should we market now? We have more business coming in the door than we can handle. Our phone is ringing off the hook." *Why* would you want to motivate your partners and staff to help grow your firm if you are already busy?

What Smart Partners Say

Here's what the top partners of many of America's leading CPA and legal firms tell me.

- "Now is the best time to train the future owners of our firms to grow the practice. We have the cash flow to invest in marketing and training."
- "During good times, we must become very selective as to the new clients we take. We must restrain ourselves to accept only the cream of the callers."
- "During good times, we can afford to outsource some of our low end clients and add clients who are more profitable and fun to work with."
- "During good times and staff shortages, some of our competitors are not giving the best in client service. Some of these clients can be persuaded to come try us out."

What Smart Associates and Staff Say

- "By learning to market, I can have more control over whether I make partner or not."
- "If I just stay in the 'back room' and do the work, I will only

be one-dimensional as a professional and won't be contributing fully to the firm."

- "The easiest way to get to do the kind of work I like, instead of whatever I happen to be assigned, is to develop the work myself. Besides, I like to think that certain clients are 'mine.'"

- "As staff, my own job security and bonuses are better if I work for professionals who are doing well."

- "Things are more interesting around here when there are new clients with new problems instead of the same old stuff."

- "When I make myself more valuable by cultivating relationships with clients and handling routine stuff myself, I feel better about myself AND I get more recognition and rewards."

Conclusion

Take a cue from our profession's leaders and develop your personal marketing skills. When you become a professional who can also market, you will be the master of your destiny.

2 Are You a Top Rainmaker?

According to a Harvard Business School study, the best rainmakers in professional firms have certain characteristics. Most of the characteristics are the result of learning, not genetics. Most professionals can be rainmakers. If you are willing to study, practice, and focus on improving your selling performance, you can be a rainmaker.

Evaluate yourself, and ask your partners to evaluate themselves on the following six attributes. Commit to an improvement program where there might be weaknesses.

Willingness to Spend Time to Develop "Like and Trust"

Businesspeople conduct business with people they like and trust. They won't do business with you if they don't like you, no matter how great a professional you are. If you are unwilling to personally meet with prospects, your prospects don't have a chance to develop "like" with you. And, even though you are honest to the core, communicating ambiguity, uncertainty, or an unwillingness to take a position does not engender trust.

Acceptance of Responsibility for Results

Too many people use a variation of the old line, "The dog ate my homework." The best rainmakers take full responsibility for results. If you don't succeed at winning the new account, don't blame the economy or your partners. Instead, when you don't meet with success, work harder to turn the negatives to your advantage later.

Above Average Willpower and Ambition

The Harvard study concluded that self-discipline is a key for top sellers to succeed. Any person who has the willpower to master the knowledge needed to pass the CPA or bar exam has an enormous amount of ambition and self-discipline. No matter how tempted top sellers were to give up, they persisted toward goals.

Intense Goal Orientation

For you to be a top rainmaker, you must make this a goal in your business life.

Ability to Approach Strangers

Every seller has some level of call reluctance. But the best rainmakers train themselves to overcome the butterflies and get out of the office and meet people.

High Level of Empathy

Until you are able to put yourself in your client's shoes, imagine their needs and concerns, and then respond appropriately, you will only be a minor league rainmaker.

Conclusion

Now ask yourself: How did I rate as a rainmaker? What should I be doing to improve my selling ability?

3 Visionaries Plan for Success

Without plans, most individuals and firms fail at marketing before they even begin. Plans provide goals for your growth. Plans provide your investment a purpose and a return. Without a plan, you will end up wherever you happen to wander.

Visions Are Realistic

A good personal or firm plan must begin with a vision of what you want your business to look like in some distant time. A vision is reality in the future—this is different than a dream. Your vision of a future business state usually entails producing top-line revenue. So, revenue is a great place to start. What is the total amount of revenue in your future state? You may want to visualize the revenue in service categories or markets.

The vision you have established is your "What." Once you can visualize your "What," then develop your "Why." Why do you want to grow to a certain size? Is it to provide you a better life? Provide better service to more clients? Create a firm that can be passed on to another generation of professionals? If you have a strong "Why," you can accomplish almost any "What."

With a vision of the future, you must set forth action plans that will likely lead to your desired result. Use action plans that include steps such as involvement in a trade group, writing articles in important journals, speaking at industry meetings, and meeting with important targeted clients and prospects.

Action Needs Vision

Many professionals begin their plans with the *action steps*. This is a huge mistake. When you begin your plan with the action steps, you will not have the motivation to carry out the steps. Having a firm grip on a solid and important vision will provide the motivation to keep going when circumstances weaken your drive.

Remember, though, all plans are dynamic, not carved-in-stone documents. Be prepared to reach for unexpected opportunities. All plans begin with intended strategy. But circumstances will prove that certain actions do not work. Other circumstances will give rise to opportunities you did not consider. With a dynamic plan, your realized strategy will be a happy ending.

Summary

Remember that marketing is an investment activity. What you do with your billable time determines your income this year. What you do with your marketing is an investment in your future income. As part of your marketing plan, clearly set forth the amount of time and dollars you are willing to invest. Make sure the amounts invested make sense as related to your intended result.

Finally, it's not what you know about marketing or what you plan to do about marketing that counts. It is your commitment to marketing *action* that will achieve results for you.

Note: See Appendix A for an outline of a sample marketing plan items.

4 Motivating Employees for Marketing

Do you want better sales results from associates? A partner told me recently, "We've had a bonus plan for years and no one seems to care." If this is true of your firm, perhaps it's time to rethink your compensation plan.

If you pay staff members a flat salary for hours worked, then you will get just that: hours. An imaginative bonus plan will stimulate employees to help attract and retain clients.

Finding and retaining loyal employees is one of the secrets to marketing success. When you create pay plans that are imaginative and fun, and when you can tap into other motivators such as recognition and family support, you will keep your best people and keep them excited about their work. They can also help you recruit more people like them.

I have researched this concept thoroughly over the past few years with many firms and other consultants. We have found five characteristics of incentive pay plans that create success.

Reward for Effort

Jay Conrad Levinson says it takes an average of 27 marketing attempts to move a prospect to readiness to engage. Keeping momentum in a long sales cycle is important, but difficult. No wonder most people give up after the second or third attempt. It is the cumulative effect of repeated marketing efforts that yields new clients. Firms that reward effort create an environment that encourages staffers to build relationships that can pay off in the long term.

Rewarding effort need not break the bank. Let your associates know that at least half of their bonuses and raises depend on marketing *efforts.*

Reward the Results Your Associates Can Control

Don't wait for the client to pay the bill. Pay for creating the lead. Pay them even if the lead does not become a new client. Initiating introductions to qualified prospects is a valuable habit for you to support.

Pay bonuses for regular attendance at civic and business club meetings.

Make Rewards Timely

Quickly reward the effort and results you want repeated. Again, don't wait till the client pays. Quick rewards encourage more action.

Reward Publicly and Often

If you can pass out bonus checks regularly at staff meetings, you will create excitement. When you reward publicly, you are employing a more powerful motivator than money: recognition. Being recognized by one's peers for a job well done is more long-lasting than money.

Reward with Products, Vacations, or Entertainment

Products such as televisions or trips are remembered long after cash has been spent. When you reward with tangible items you impact the employee longer and you may positively affect his or her spouse.

5 Eight Ways to Build Your Firm Over the Next 12 Months

Is this going to be your year for turning on the power of marketing and sales in your business? If your answer is yes, here are eight keys to success:

1. **Focus on the Client's Profits, Not Your Own**
   There is a limited demand for routine tax return preparation services or will preparation, but there is unlimited demand for professionals who help clients improve profits!

2. **Don't Hibernate During Compliance Season**
   Clients are never more interested in help with their business than when confronted with last year's financial results or with their tax liability. Plan now for cross-selling to each client you meet with during this filing season. Augment the effort with preprepared press releases, articles, and mailings.

3. **Build Relationships with Your Clients' Team Members**
   This year, plan to meet with your top 10 clients' other professionals. These people are the movers and shakers in your community. By creating a team working for your client, you will also have created a referral team that works for you.

4. **Develop a Unique Selling Proposition, and Quit Talking about Fees**
   When meeting with prospects, focus on the value you can offer, and on what makes you different from your competitors. Fee terms should almost be an afterthought.

5. Learn to Ask Better Questions

Knowing how to ask good questions is the foundation of being an effective advisor. Through questioning, you learn what you need to know to help your clients.

6. Help Clients Prepare for the Future

Clients are more interested in today and tomorrow than they are in yesterday. Help your clients use your services as a foundation for making better judgments and business decisions.

7. Prepare a Services Matrix

Prepare a matrix of your largest clients and services used. Probably 5% of your clients (including families and controlled groups) make up over 50% of your revenue. Use the matrix to determine your best opportunities.

8. Always Give More Than You Promise

Always exceed your client expectations by 1% and you will have a continuous flow of delighted clients. Sometimes, under pressure, you may promise delivery of a report before it can realistically be done. Learn to manage expectations by promising the outside date, not the earliest. Then deliver earlier.

Prospecting

6 Consultant's Advice Spells Disaster: Instead, All Strategy Begins with the Market

I had the challenge of working with a large firm whose growth had flattened out during the preceding three years. (In contrast, in the previous five years the firm had experienced double-digit growth.) Owner earnings in the most recent two years had decreased. During our strategic assessment process, I learned that the firm had engaged a well-known strategic planner prior to the three-year decline and had followed his advice.

"Standard" Advice for Squeezing Profits and Quality

What advice had this planner given the firm? It boiled down to this:

- In order to improve partner earnings, you should increase partner charge hours.
- Decrease the hiring process and focus on high chargeable hours from your staff.
- Use technology more to help reduce the size of the administrative staff. Instead of one administrative person for every owner, reduce it to one for every three.
- Delay investments in technology to replace systems every five years rather than every three.
- Bring all training in-house.

This highly regarded strategic planner had given the firm a plan for disaster. Short-term profits were squeezed from training, technology, and marketing. Within only three years, the prospect pipeline dried up and the owner's computer network had become "clunky" compared to what was now available. While owner profits soared for two years, by the third year profits began to slide as the owners worked harder than ever.

The owners were now looking inward, rather than out to the market.

Work with the Market

Successful strategic planning should always begin with the market outside the firm, not the internal processes inside the firm. Yet, when owners retreat to discuss strategic plans, the agenda items frequently include staff evaluations, raises and bonuses, owner compensation, admission of new owners, the financial results for last year, the budget for next year, new office space, recruiting efforts, and other issues that do not fall into true strategic planning.

Conclusion

Just as your "market" is more than your clients, strategy must be more than a way to get more profits in the short-term. Strategy should focus on building the balance sheet of your firm so profits will be strong for the long term. When setting the agenda for your firm's strategic planning session, first start with the market, then look internally.

7 Turning Prospects into Clients

Good marketing programs create many prospects. But all prospects do not—and should not—convert to clients. Here are ideas to help you convert prospects into clients.

Take Action Immediately

Not immediately following up with prospects causes them to go cold. Then you are right back where you started. The prospect will likely forget meeting you. Or, the prospect may think you are not interested in serving her. Furthermore, your response time to a lead's request is an indication of your response time when he is a client. So take action quickly when you receive a telephone inquiry, a trade-show lead, a referral, or other lead.

Focus on Referrals

Referred prospects are the most valuable. When you receive a referred lead, the selling has already been done. If you act quickly on referred leads, it will reflect well on your source, and he will be inclined to refer you again. If you delay on a referred lead or handle it poorly, don't expect to receive any further leads from your valuable referrer.

Evaluate the Lead

Some follow-up on every lead is a good idea. You want to separate the suspects from the prospects. Evaluating the lead will enable you to follow up more quickly with the better prospects. Ask the lead or the referral source about problems, needs and wants, the decision process, and his or her ability to pay your fees. Ask these questions as early in the process as you can.

Have a Follow-up Plan

An automatic follow-up system will make it easy for you to follow up in the same way every time.

Set aside a definite time for contacting and courting a new prospect. Unless you set aside time in your calendar, you may have trouble fitting it in. Prospect value can dissipate rapidly. If you are fully booked, fire off a letter or call the lead to set a specific time to meet.

Add the Prospect to a Mail List

Every professional should have a marketing database. When you obtain a lead, the information should be permanently recorded in your database. "A" prospects should receive regular and personal attention, whereas "C" prospects can be handled by mail. (Handling of "B" prospects can depend on your load.)

Give the Prospect to Someone Else

If you cannot follow up the prospect, or if the lead is of little interest to you, give it to someone else in your firm. Selling is a team effort. Ask your designee to keep you informed as to the progress of the prospect. Offer to help when the prospect gets close to closing.

Conclusion

A pipeline full of good prospects is critical to the steady growth of a firm. A full pipeline enables you to be selective and to follow up with the best leads.

8 The "R" Word . . .

Rejection isn't really rejection unless you accept it as final! Much research has shown that moving a prospect from contact to contract will take about nine positive marketing interactions with your firm. You might think of the first eight attempts as rejections, but they're not. The reality is that many of your attempted interactions are missed by your prospects. And just because they don't buy now doesn't mean they won't later.

Ross Perot said it took him 68 sales calls before he made his first sale for EDS in 1962. He built two major companies in the process. Colonel Sanders (KFC) didn't sell a "franchise" until he'd talked to over 1,000 restaurants.

When a prospect doesn't hire you early, he is not rejecting you. People have different circumstances and different timetables for making decisions.

You Can Deal With "Nonsuccess"

A technique to help you overcome the fear of rejection is: Don't go for the kill on the first call. Set the objective for the first interaction at a very low level, maybe just creating awareness. If you can then build each successive call into a gradual sales strategy, then your fear of rejection won't stop you.

Another technique is planning your response to rejection. Your contact may have a rational reason for not doing business with you right now. Your contact may be having a bad day and her lackluster response is not your fault.

Persistence Pays

A steady, consistent approach will win out every time. The average sale in American commerce is made on the fifth sales call, but the average professional makes only two or three calls. Because the buying cycle is long and unpredictable, the average professional services sale may take over a dozen contacts. Yet many professionals let their fear of rejection keep them from ever getting started!

Professionals are trained to avoid making mistakes. However, when you view marketing as a numbers game, the impact of rejection will be less. The feeling of rejection you have when someone does not hire you immediately can be depressing. However, if you approach the market with the realization that over 90% of your marketing activity will not pay off today, you gain a more realistic perspective.

Summary

Remind yourself that marketing that is not successful today can be successful tomorrow. Activity will help build a good client relationship. Engage in positive self-talk and separate your ego from the sale. When you can accept temporary nonsuccess, you will be a stronger professional who can market.

Last, maintain a healthy balance between positive client interaction and new prospect activity. The client relationships will enable you to be confident with prospects.

9 The Seven Deadly Sins of Prospecting

Looking for new clients needs to be a regular and ongoing effort. No matter how good your retention rate, there will be some attrition and need to upgrade your client base.

Prospecting is much like exercising or practicing your golf swing. Until your business goes flat you aren't aware of the neglect. Here are the seven deadly sins of prospecting. Avoid them like the plague:

1. **No System for Prospecting**

   Most professional firms have systems for paying the bills and systems for collecting accounts receivable. Every firm needs a system for collecting, and following up on prospects.

2. **No Qualifying of Prospects**

   Prospects who are interested, but who are not qualified to do business with you, will waste your time and your money. Qualify the prospect by asking the questions necessary to ensure the prospect will make a profitable client.

3. **No Consistency in Prospecting**

   Successful prospecting requires discipline. Professionals tend to prospect heavily at the same time all their competitors are prospecting. Consistent prospecting systems will help you build on the power of compound impressions and on being in front of prospects when they are ready to buy.

4. No Organization to Prospecting

I use a computer contact system to manage thousands of contacts and I strongly recommend you use one as well. ACT, Telemagic, and Goldmine are three systems that are well-tested and sound.

5. No Scripting for Prospecting Calls

You should have a routine you follow with every prospecting call. If you have a script, you'll be reminded of the right questions, and the right things to say.

6. No Follow-up to a Prospect Inquiry

Recently, I called three air-conditioning companies within one hour and did business with the first one who made an appointment. If you ignore a prospect call for an hour, you may lose it.

7. No Research on the Prospect

In all businesses, there are several decision makers. Usually, there is someone who has "big YES" authority and others who have "little yes" and "big NO" authority. Doing your homework on the players helps you avoid getting the "big NO" before the "big YES."

Summary

A solid system of prospecting will help your firm grow consistently through good times and bad. Avoid the seven deadly sins and prosper with your prospects.

10 Trade Shows Can Create Good Leads

Willie Sutton had the right idea. Asked why he robbed banks, the infamous bandit replied, "Because that's where the money is."

Prospecting for leads isn't quite as easy as finding money in a bank. But if you're seeking to fill your sales hopper full of good prospects, it makes sense to exhibit at an industry trade show.

Here are a few pointers to help you make your trade show a winner.

Focus on the Result

You want to end up with new clients as a result of your trade show activity. Realistically, the trade show encounter is only the first step in about nine marketing interactions that you should plan with a new prospect BEFORE he or she will engage you.

Coming away with good leads often requires you to evaluate the trade show's potential for generating the right leads. Ask the show promoter for a list of last year's exhibitors and call two or three of them to find out the "rest of the story."

Rarely will your attendance at a show result in immediate business. According to Kathryn Clark, writing in *Personal Selling Power* magazine, "two thirds of all sales from trade shows aren't achieved until 11 to 24 months after a show." So set a realistic expectation for lead generation.

Know What Types of Leads You Want

Before you attend the show, decide what type of lead you will seek. For example, when you attend a trade show for your primary industry niche, the attendees at the show may be your predetermined targets. Other times, at a general business exhibit, the exhibitors themselves may be your targets.

Every time you meet someone at the trade show, attempt to qualify him or her as a potential prospect. Ask planned questions that will enable you to follow up appropriately after the show. Ask pertinent questions about their current provider, such as: Has your professional helped you be more profitable? Has your accountant helped you deal with new technology? Has your attorney helped you with business advice?

> *When you plan your trade show booth, consider a unique theme that will attract potential prospects. We recently did a plant shop theme where we decorated our booth like a florist shop and used the motto "We help you grow your business." Our giveaway was a small plant with our logo on the planter. Many attendees stopped at our booth just because it was different. We have a reputation for changing our theme each year, so many attendees actually search our booth out. The lesson here is to differentiate yourself! (We also won an award for this idea at the 2002 Association for Accounting Marketing convention.)*
> —Deborah Bailey Browne, Partner with Vanacore,
> DeBenedictus, DiGovanni & Weddell

Conclusion

If you are well prepared, trade shows can be an effective vehicle for professionals who are willing to reach out to people in a show environment.

11 Broad-Based Marketing Supports Prospecting

Mass media (radio, TV, national publications) reach a large number of people, most of whom aren't potential clients. Rather, you should be very targeted with your selection of media and try to achieve personal contact as soon as possible.

Advertising and Public Relations

Advertising and public relations are usually best when included in targeted trade or industry publications. Advertising is an expensive technique for attracting prospects. Only those firms whose marketing is sophisticated and mature will benefit from a significant advertising budget.

Smaller firms and professionals are better off focusing on public relations for media exposure. Writing articles for your trade journal or business newspaper is a good way to become known in a community of prospects. Readers generally perceive an article to be five times more believable than advertising.

Public relations can also be executed in the form of press releases, sponsorships of events, speaking opportunities, and other activities.

Newsletters

Targeted direct mail is usually very effective because the print media can be directed at your best prospects, clients, and referral sources. Newsletters are a form of direct mail that contains professional advice, observations, and comment. Regular newsletters keep your name in front of your prospects and remind them to contact you when a need arises. Specialty trade newsletters attract the serious reader to do more than recognize your name. Firms that write their own newsletters have excellent client responses. But the publication process can be daunting. So most firms use some form of prepackaged newsletter program. Practice Development Institute, Chicago, and M. Lee Smith, Nashville, are the leading publishers of newsletters for accountants, lawyers, and financial advisors.

Websites

Most people in today's modern world receive much of their information electronically through television, radio, and the Internet. It makes good sense to have a website. Your website can take the form of an electronic brochure, with articles and other credibility builders. People who are interested in you will check out your website. If it is good, a favorable impression can be made before meetings. If it is not good, you might have difficulty gaining serious interest.

Conclusion

Services are bought and sold by personal contact. Broad-based marketing should be designed to create it.

12 Tip Clubs

Any time you network with other people, you can get a business lead or referral. For instance, industry associations can work as tip clubs if you make the effort to network. However, specific groups called tips groups or clubs have been created for members to give other members leads and referrals.

There are many variations on tips groups, but generally you attend weekly and bring in a lead for someone else in the group. Groups typically limit membership to one of each type of business so that there is no competition. This means there may not be an opening in established groups if they already have an accountant or attorney.

Start Your Own Group?

Stockbrokers, insurance agents, bonding agents, bankers, and many other professionals are looking for referrals. Consider forming a "tip" or "lead" group. You could ask a bank trust officer, a computer vendor, an insurance broker, a commercial real estate developer, and other compatible professionals to join your club.

Think about your clients first as potential members, then their service providers and bankers. While groups usually have 20 or so members, even a very small group can work if you get people who bring you regular leads.

Existing Franchises

If you don't want to start your own group, there are many groups available, including franchises (Business Network International, Le Tip, Leads Club) and groups run by your local Chambers of Commerce.

Conclusion

You can often find existing tips groups listed in your local newspaper business calendars. Such groups can give you a structure to improve your prospecting and referrals many times over.

CHAPTER
THREE

Qualifying

13 Big Hat, No Cattle

Texans call people who live the life of the rich and famous, without real wealth, "big hat, no cattle." Take notice of the people with whom you are networking. Do they have the resources to pay your fees and grow with you or are they "big hat, no cattle?"

In *The Millionaire Next Door,* authors Thomas J. Stanley and William D. Danko assert that the typical millionaire has a boring business and can be met in a trade association. Most millionaires do not flash their wealth. Rather, the authors found, "People who look like they are living the good life may not have much wealth."

Finding Wealthy Prospects

The book points out that very often those who supply the wealthy become wealthy themselves. The authors state, "There are significant opportunities for those who target the affluent, the children of the affluent, and the widows and widowers of the affluent." They estimate hundreds of billions of tax dollars will be paid to the federal government during the next 10 years. Professionals advising families and serving estates will earn huge fees to help conserve as much wealth as possible.

The science of qualifying starts with the segment of the market you select for networking and communicating.

Segmenting your market into least likely, possible, and most likely categories will assist you in deciding where to invest your networking time. Prospecting a target-rich segment of the market just makes good sense.

Stanley and Danko's research is comforting news for professionals who are networking in trade associations. They sent out 3,000 questionnaires to affluent Americans and conducted about 100 in-person interviews. Their findings build on some of Stanley's earlier research, published in his book *Marketing to the Affluent*. About two thirds of working millionaires are self-employed and own mundane businesses like scrap metal, welding, highway construction, and dry cleaning.

The wealthy list their CPAs and attorneys as their trusted business advisors. The millionaires list tax shelters, disciplined investing, and extreme thriftiness as keys to their amassing real wealth.

Conclusion

How can you profit from the advice in this book? First, make one of your priorities to aggressively network with your affluent clients and acquaintances. If necessary, give up time you are spending with less-promising clients. Second, pay attention to the next generation of owners of your clients' businesses. When the business ownership and management changes, you don't want them changing professionals.

Third, become involved in an industry trade association. Most affluent business owners value their trade associations above all other organizations. Fourth, become an advocate of the wealthy. Write your senators and legislators on matters that can help your clients. (Send a copy of letters to your affluent prospects and clients with a note saying, "This is an issue that probably affects you.")

14 NEAD-PAY

NEAD-PAY is an acronym (slightly misspelled) for a pattern of asking qualifying questions. When you religiously follow this pattern, you will have a good idea about the prospect's qualification to do business with you.

N stands for *Now*. Ask the prospect "Who are you using *now* for your advice?" The answer to this question tells you the names of your competition and perhaps the names of other advisors. When you know the names of the entrenched competitor, you may have some idea about their reputation, clients, and personnel. Another question to ask might be, "What are you doing *now* about your legal protection (or your tax situation)?"

E stands for *Enjoy*. Ask the prospect, "What do you *enjoy* or like about your present accountant or lawyer?" Or ask it another way: "Do you feel good when you are working with your professional?" or "What do you like most about X?" When you ask questions about what is good about your competitor, you relax the prospect. You also may receive some insight into the next question.

A stands for *Alter*. Ask the prospect, "What would you *alter* about the service you receive?" Or you could ask, "If you had the perfect relationship with your professional, what would you *alter* to make you perfectly happy?" Prospects' motivation to change to you is created by your making them dissatisfied with the status quo.

D stands for *Decision*. Ask questions about the *decision* process, the *decision* makers, and the *decision* criteria. Questions like, "Who, besides you, is involved in the *decision* to hire a law firm?" Or, "The last time you changed accountants, how did you go about the process?"

PAY stands for *payment,* budget, or money. A good question around this point might look something like this: "Bill, our firm has many clients who engage us because they want the very best and money is no object. Others hire us to do a job for them, but they know we can serve in a variety of ways. Some few clients really watch the pennies. What type of client might you be?"

If this question seems too abrupt to you, it is because you haven't established enough rapport with the prospect at this point. You must use finesse in asking these questions. You may want to keep the interaction conversational. You might even find it better to ask these questions over a series of meetings.

Conclusion

Prospects buy emotionally and justify with logic. Therefore, as you progress in the qualification process, you must get at the emotional reasons a prospect has for hiring you. NEAD-PAY is a way to uncover transactional or logical information. If you can uncover the emotional hot buttons, such as comfort or prestige, you will have information that will help you close the sale.

Don't stop with the answers to these questions. Keep asking more questions and nurture your prospects with every question.

15 Too Busy to Grow?

Is your firm running at capacity? Do you think that what you need is a few more associates with 5 to 10 years' experience, not more business? If this is you, you probably haven't done a good job of qualifying your clients. A key objective of good marketing is to attract *better* clients, not just *more* business.

Highly qualified clients usually have benefits for you in four areas: more profits, more fun, more leisure, and more learning.

More Profit

Evaluate the relative profitability of each client. List your clients from largest discount to largest premium in size categories, and by season. Apply a cost factor to each client and then re-sort the clients based on total profit per client. Then select the least profitable 5% of your client base. You should dramatically increase pricing on these clients or outplace them to another service provider.

Value Pricing

The best method to increase your profits is to improve the value of your service and to price your service based on value. Professionals who focus on creating client value yield high profits for themselves.

More Fun

You have more fun when you work with clients you enjoy. It might be their personalities, the types of issues, or their industries. It might be novelty.

Some clients just don't fit your personal style, or are all around difficult types. Consider dropping at least one undesirable client. Your professional life will be more fun.

Aggressively pursue a new client who you think will be more fun. Now is a great time to upgrade your fun quotient.

More Leisure

For most people, their most productive work occurs after a period of rest, not after having worked ten 15-hour days straight. Exhausting yourself creates burnout, low creativity, and poor staff relations.

Prepare your calendar with days of leisure included. Don't violate your planned "free" days. Your professional days will be more productive and satisfying.

More Skill Growth

I've met professionals in their 40s and 50s who are bored to tears with their work lives. The main reason seems to be because they have been doing the same thing for 25 years. In contrast, professionals who continue to build skills seem to enjoy their professions deep into their 50s, 60s, and 70s.

Conclusion

A successful firm is about more than gross billings. By selecting the right clients, you can have more profits *and* more fun.

16 Use the "David Letterman" Dismissal for Unqualified Clients and Prospects

Ever watch David Letterman dismiss a guest on his show? He simply stands up, looks the guest in the eye, shakes his hand and says, "Thanks for stopping by; good luck with your new movie."

Firing Clients

You may have many clients who are really unqualified to do business with you. Clients who don't pay the bills on time, who require more service than they pay for, and who irritate you and your staff.

If you fire the client, you stand the chance of antagonizing him. If your client leaves angry, he will tell many other people in your community. Why not arrange for your unqualified client to meet with another professional who can serve the client's need well? Once you have made the introductions and explained the benefits of these two working together, stand up, look the former client in the eye, shake her hand and say, "Thanks for being my client, good luck with Bob. I know he will really take care of you."

Networking

The same situation holds true when you are networking at a business mixer or trade show. You can waste a lot of time chatting with unqualified prospects. In fact, the more unqualified the prospect is, the more he seems to linger around you. So what do you do?

First, make it a rule to not give any unqualified prospect more than two minutes of your time at a networking event or trade show. Second, say, "Thanks for stopping by, I hope you enjoy the evening." Third, turn and move on to the next person in line, or step across the room and "capture" a more qualified looking person.

Conclusion

Using a series of qualifying questions will enable you to determine quickly if this person is qualified to do business with you. Many people you meet will not be. Use the David Letterman dismissal and invest your time with prospects who are qualified.

FOUR

Gaining Access to Decision Makers

17 Reaching Decision Makers

When making initial contact with the people who make or influence decisions, we have two key tactics to consider before the approach: (1) Will we make a warm or a cold contact? and (2) Which decision influencer will we target first?

Warm Calls

When making a first contact, the openness of the prospect will be improved if you are able to make a warm contact. Warm means that the prospect already knows something about you from one of her trusted friends or advisors. It means the prospect's interest has been warmed up before you meet.

In The Rainmaker Academy, we teach students that a good way to warm up a lead is to ask one of your mutual friends to introduce you and tell the prospect something positive about you. If the friend has a strong advisory relationship with the prospect, all the better. Another way would be to have someone you know inside the company introduce you.

Ask Permission

There are still many prospects where you cannot find a mutual acquaintance to introduce you. You can still warm up the lead with a permission marketing campaign. Seth Godin's book, *Permission Marketing*, describes most marketing as "interruption marketing." Commercials that interrupt your television program, ads that break up the flow of reading your magazine, or the telephone interrupting your evening dinner are all examples of interruption marketing. Godin recommends asking permission to make an offer, or promising a reward for the prospect's response as a more respectful way to build a relationship with a prospect before you meet. Godin likens permission marketing to dating—when dating, you make incremental advances toward a relationship.

Multiple Contacts

As you target larger businesses, the decision-making power is not as clear as in smaller units. As the decision making becomes more complex, decision power is spread among more people.

When your prospect is a larger business, you are often better off starting your sales approach with a person who is more accessible or approachable than the CEO. With an approachable and receptive person, you will be able to gather important information about the business, its problems, and its politics. Building a strong relationship with the receptive insider can lead to a strong introduction to the ultimate decision maker. Armed with valuable information coupled with an insider's introduction, you will make the time you have with the CEO more valuable.

Conclusion

When possible, start with warm leads. Ask for referrals when they are available. Otherwise, start relationships by asking permission.

18 Tips to Help You Gain Access to Decision Makers

The best way to gain access to decision makers is through warm referrals, but you can use nonreferral prospecting to build a cadre of great clients. Use the following techniques to gain access to those key decision makers.

Use Local News

Clip photos and news articles about your prospects and send them to the prospect with a note. This will gain you receptivity points once you meet.

For big impact, take the clipping to a professional framer and have the material placed under glass in an attractive frame. Then deliver the framed news article to the prospect with a congratulatory note. Such an unusual approach will likely get you a phone call thank you.

Take a Celebrity to Meet the Prospect

Will you have an out of town expert visiting you this year? Ask the celebrity to make some visits with you to important prospects. You could arrange a luncheon or breakfast with several clients and prospects together and have private meetings for your top few prospects.

Short on celebrities? Take the managing partner or a niche expert or a tax expert to visit several of your top prospects. You could say something like this: "Our managing partner will be working with me on Tuesday and Wednesday next week and he would like to meet you. Which day would be good for a meeting?"

Take Advantage of Turnover

Whenever you hear about an impending staff change in one of your top prospects' businesses, brainstorm ways you could help. Call the key decision maker and ask if the person leaving will be replaced. If the response is "yes," offer to be of help. If the position is a financial or legal position, offer to provide assistance with one of your associates until the new hire is in place.

Snow Days Are Good Access Times

Do you live in an area that gets snowed in? Decision makers are usually the last ones to leave the office. When the boss is in his office without receptionists and screeners, your phone call will likely get through. Your chances of getting decision-making prospects on the phone during off business hours, such as snow days, are very good.

Leave Enticing Voicemails at Odd Hours

When you have solved a problem for a top client or learn of a unique method for making more profits, call those prospects who would benefit from the information at 11 P.M. and say something like, "Bill, I have an interesting idea to help you make more profits from your business this year. I just helped another client with this and he saved $120,000 in taxes. Call me at 555-1212 and lets get together and see if you can benefit too."

Your prospect will hear the voice mail the next morning and will think, "This person left a message on my system at 11 P.M.

What kind of crazy person is thinking of me at 11 P.M.? He had some ideas. Maybe I'd better call and get with him."

19 Your Message Is the Lure, Your Promise Is the Hook

Crafting a message that will appeal to your best prospects' emotional interests will stimulate interest in your services. Every day, prospects are bombarded by sales messages. A strong emotional message will help you attract good prospects to your firm.

How do you craft such a message? Most clients want a relationship of trust with their accountant, consultant, or attorney. In their book *The Discipline of Market Leaders,* Michael Treacy and Fred Wiersema explained that you can't be all things to all people. You must first understand what your best customers value. Do your clients engage you because you are the lowest priced? Because you have the best technical skills or software? Or do your clients most value the relationship with you because you solve their problems? For many professional firms, the last question is the appropriate one.

If you perform traditional research, you might learn that your clients want fast, accurate, reasonably priced work. But it is important to dig below the surface to learn what clients want that is different, better, or special.

Start the Relationship with a Promise

Once you have a good message in place, then find a way to make a promise and keep it. For example, you should have about 20 articles, newsletters, or brochures that address the common issues that interest your best clients. Then when you meet a solid qualified prospect, offer to send one of the articles relevant to the concerns of the person you have just met. By keeping your promise, you now have the basis for a solid telephone follow-up. During the telephone follow-up call, make another promise and keep it.

What if the prospect doesn't say, "Come on over and let's talk"? What if your offers are rebuked? Then you must develop a better offer. Too many professionals are rebuffed when they offer to meet with the prospect for a free hour. It is not the job of the prospect to give you his time. It is your job to make such an irresistible offer that he wants it.

Conclusion

One of the keys to successful selling is to market to people who desire communication. So invest some time to craft your message and create your offers. Make the good prospects offers they can't refuse.

20 Speaking Helps Open Doors

A few years ago, I heard Brian Tracy say that people perceive how much you know on a subject by the way you communicate. If you write well on a subject, people infer that you know four times what you really may know, whereas if you speak to groups, people think that you know 10 times as much.

You Can Be a Communicator

The computer takes care of much of the mundane number and contract crunching. Lawyers are becoming contract communicators. Accountants are becoming number communicators rather than number crunchers. Clients want to know, "How does this affect me?"

Speaking to groups will hone your oral communication skills and will help position you as an expert on the topic. When you develop a reputation as an expert, you will be more welcome in the executive offices of many of your best prospects. Speaking will help open many doors for you.

Small meetings and seminars have proven over the years to be great venues for meeting and following up with decision makers and influencers in important prospects. It just makes good sense—a small meeting allows you to give more one-on-one time to a prospect and speak directly to her issues.

Getting prospects to your meeting starts with a good title. A topic like "the legal implications of labor contracts" is boring. Try a more interesting title like one of the following:

- "Increase Your Profits NOW by Giving Your Employees a Raise"

- "The IRS Wants Your Money: How the Self-Employed Can Keep Taxes Low"
- "Raise Millions in New Capital: How to Attract Money in the Capital Markets"
- "Right-Sizing Your Workforce Without Inviting Litigation"

Running the Seminar

Before giving a seminar, make sure the room is comfortable. You can have a stellar performance, but if your prospects are physically uncomfortable, it will negatively impact your response.

The best way to stimulate enthusiasm in the room is to create a dialogue among the participants. You should speak no longer than about 20 minutes, then ask for table discussions and feedback. Make certain that your associates are strategically placed at the participant's tables, not standing in the back of the room like birds on a telephone wire.

Build in Follow-up

During your presentation, make reference to materials you have available for those interested. Don't pass the materials out at the meeting, ask people to give you their business cards and you will get the material to them. Your follow-up to these requests can vary. For example, you could mail the material requested to low-level prospects and hand deliver the material to top prospects.

Note: See Appendix B for a Checklist for deciding on a seminar, workshop, or training program.

Identifying Decision Influencers

21 There Are No Single Decision Makers

A few years ago, I purchased a toy for my son. I had invested an hour or so trying it out and talking to the clerk at Toys-R-Us, and was proud of the decision I had made. The sales clerk thought he had made a sale. But to my surprise and disappointment, my son wasn't interested in the toy at all. He didn't thank me or acknowledge my hard work. As it turned out, a couple of his friends had the same toy and hated it.

A few days later, I returned the toy to the store. The pride of my decision making was extinguished. Both the sales clerk and I learned a valuable selling lesson that day: to make a sale requires that all decision influencers come to terms with the decision.

Dealing with Multiple Decision Makers

So it goes in the businesses we serve. There are few decision makers, only decision influencers. From the smallest business to the largest organization, decisions to engage your services are made by multiple individuals.

As the businesses to which you are selling grow larger, the number of decision influencers increases. As the number of influencers increases, the complexity of the sale grows. To improve your selling success in large organizations, you must identify and persuade all the decision influencers.

The relative power held by a person in a particular position in one company usually will be quite different in another organization. The decision process and the relative power of specific decision influencers can vary greatly in businesses of the same type and size.

Conclusion

When selling to organizations, it is crucial to identify and persuade *all* the decision influencers. Professionals who routinely cover only one of the decision influencers sell substantially less than their share of the business. For example, a professional who makes 10 proposals and has two competitors on each should sell one in three, or 33%, if he is getting his share. However, we find that sellers who meet with only one buying influencer will get a 10–15% share while sellers who meet with several decision influencers score in the 40% to 70% range.

22 Identifying the Major Decision Influencers

Identifying the major decision influencers is a crucial step in the selling process. Develop your prowess in the group dynamics of complex decision making and you will be the all-star of new business development in your firm.

There are many identifiable decision influencers in a business. They include the executive, the user, the outsider, and the deal killer.

The Executive

The executive influencer is the person with the most power in the decision to engage you. This person has "big YES" authority. "Big YES" authority means that this person listens to all the recommendations from others and makes the final decision to hire you. The larger the financial commitment to hire you, the more likely it is that strong power resides in a top executive. When small dollars and limited services are involved, executive power can reside in the user. If you do not obtain an audience with the executive decision influencer, your chances of making the sale diminish rapidly.

The User

The user is the person in your prospect's businesses who will interact with you and most frequently use your services directly. In-house counsel, corporate controllers, and risk managers are a few of the possible users.

Since the user is going to be interacting with you the most and it's to the business's benefit that the user get along with you and feel comfortable with you, the other influencers often give a good deal of weight to the user's recommendation. However, others on the team may be hiring you to supplement the skills of the user or to help outplace and hire a new user. The user influencer will almost always have "big NO" authority and "little yes" authority.

The Outsider

Most companies have several outsiders that influence any decision to engage a major professional firm. Investment bankers, commercial bankers, surety bonding agents, outside board members, family members, and other professionals are some.

Outsiders usually have "big NO" authority. In many cases, the outsider can be a strong "YES" influence on the executive influencer when referring you into the opportunity.

The Deal Killer

In every organization, there lurks a person who has "big NO" authority. That person evaluates you or your firm on a set of technical standards and says to the others that you pass or fail. This person's sole job is to screen out the professionals who do not measure up. You must identify this person and learn about the set of standards he or she has set.

23 Understanding Influencers' Perceptions and Values

People make decisions emotionally and justify them with logic. But *perceptions* drive the emotions. For thousands of years, the perception that the world was flat drove the emotion of fear that kept people from sailing too far west. In any company, the perceptions of the various decision influencers may be similar or quite different. If the perceptions of individuals within an organization are radically different, the decision process will be more difficult for you to influence.

Perceptions Are Reality

If each of your decision influencers perceives that the business is in a high-growth, stimulating economy, a decision to change service providers is relatively easy. But, if some believe that economic conditions are uncertain, they will likely believe a business should hold onto its tried-and-true advisors in such times, and you may have difficulty replacing the incumbent professional.

Compare the perceptions of business among your decision influencers and look for consistencies and differences that may provide clues on how to close the sale later.

Value System

An owner of a business that was getting lousy service from their accounting firm told me, "The hardest decision I have ever made in my business career was to change accounting firms 12 years ago." That told me that his emotional "switching costs" were too high to overcome in a short few meetings. He valued loyalty and feared confronting a poorly performing professional. Such insight helped us develop a winning sales strategy that did not threaten the incumbent firm, but focused on services the client was not presently receiving.

Conclusion

During the past 20 years, I have found that a high percentage of companies who consider changing service providers keep the incumbent, when the incumbent is allowed to also propose. Beware of the "fools gold" of proposing against an incumbent.

Learn the value system of each one of your buying influences by asking lots of questions, the answers to which tell you about the values held most dear. When you understand the value systems of each person, you will be able to devise a sales strategy that has a high probability of success.

24 Understanding Influencer's Personalities

Personality styles have been studied since biblical times. The ancient Greek Hypocrites identified four distinct personalities. Others have identified many more and have concluded that everyone has several personality styles. I have learned that you can do a lot with Hypocrites' four styles: directors, compliants, influencers, and steadies. These styles are similar to a modern system called DISC.

Directors

The directors are usually quick decision makers and will allow you only a small amount of access time. They require few facts and are very bottom-line and goal-oriented. Directors live life their way. Director personalities are exhibited in a high percentage of CEOs.

Compliants

Compliants are people who measure their decisions by some internal or external set of rules. The compliant personality is a methodical decision maker and will examine many facts. Engineers, accountants, and doctors have a high percentage of compliant personalities.

Influencers

Influencers exhibit persuasive and outgoing personalities. They enjoy moving other people to their point of view. Influencers are friendly and powerful communicators. They are fast paced and have a short attention span. Influencer personalities are exhibited in many CEOs and sales managers.

Steadies

The Steady personality is a friendly person who thrives on consensus and being well liked. Steadies are usually uncomfortable with making rapid decisions. Their primary concern is for the effect of a change on other people in the organization.

Conclusion

By utilizing this knowledge of different personality types, you will be better able to present yourself in a way that is more likely to be accepted.

25 Planning Each Call Improves Success

Different decision influencers need to be approached in different ways. Forgetting to plan the objective of each sales contact or setting unrealistic objectives is the root of most sales failures. In the complex sale, a professional should plan on a series of at least five—and often as many as a dozen—personal sales calls on a large prospect. Trying to close the sale on the first call is like throwing a "Hail Mary" pass in the first quarter of a football game.

Pre-call planning will help you eliminate gaps in your knowledge about a prospect and will help you maintain the momentum necessary in a long-cycle sale. With each successive call, there should be a routine you follow to help you touch all the bases. Your contact cycle will go through a number of stages, including the following.

Research

The more you know, the better you'll do when you make your first sales call if you can answer questions like these:

- What are some common problems of companies in this industry?
- What has appeared in the press regarding this company?
- What is the content and style of the company's website?
- Who are the company's suppliers? (Consider calling them.)
- Who else works or has worked with this company? (Find out their opinions.)

During your early sales calls, you should gather additional information about the business, its problems, the decision influencers and their values, your competition, and potential service or product needs of the organization.

Focus and Track

Ask yourself, "Where am I in the sales process with this prospect?" If you are in the discovery phase, focus on the discovery issues in this book. If the prospect is in the decision phase and you are in discovery, your chances of success are limited.

Next focus on the people you know and the ones you don't know who are in the decision group. Develop a strategy to meet one or two new people on each sales call. Remember, if you are being blocked from meeting key people in the decision process, the company may not be sincere in considering you.

Conclusion

Having goals for each sales contact will focus you and improve your success rate.

Discovering Problems

26 Uncovering Prospect Problems

In order to sell services, a professional must have a command of all the potential problems of a prospect. Businesses hire professionals to help solve problems. Many of those problems are needs, but some are not.

Identifying Problems People Will Pay to Solve

Discovering problems can occur in many ways during the discovery and differentiation phase of selling. There are many ways to discover problems:

- Existing clients may have a series of problems similar to those of your prospects.
- Your prospect may belong to a trade association to help solve certain problems.
- Your prospect's problems may be discussed on the Internet.
- Your prospect may mention her problems.
- You might discover problems through a business analysis.

Before meeting with a prospect, you will find it quite helpful to review your files on similar clients or talk to your clients, associates, or partners who work on similar businesses. Your job at this point is to list as many potential problems as you possibly can.

Trade associations are excellent sources for discovering the problems associated with companies in that industry. Executives in trade associations are almost always aware of regulatory, tax, and competitive problems. You might also find industry performance statistics for an association of businesses that would apply to your prospects.

Mark Schultz, a partner with Dugan & Lopatka, uses an established process to identify client problems. It is a sophisticated benchmarking tool developed by Pricewaterhouse Coopers called the advanced middle market business intelligence tool (AMMBIT).

Conclusion

When you have created a list of all the possible problems a prospect might have, then formulate questions about the problems. Design questions that will demonstrate your knowledge of the company and its industry. This is a much more effective way of showing your knowledge than simply talking. Unless you address the problems with the prospect, in a nonjudgmental manner, your meetings will only be a low-level commercial visit.

27 Good Questions Uncover Problems

There is a major difference between good questions and average questions. Many sales experts advise you to ask "open-ended" questions. That is good advice, so long as the questions are related to a problem. To encourage prospects to tell you their problems, you may have to design powerful questions that demonstrate you are a person worthy of the answers. I like dialog questions.

Dialog Questions

Have you watched Barbara Walters interview people? She uses dialog questions to show knowledge, empathy, and sincerity, and to encourage interviewees to tell intimate details they may have never told anyone before. Asking good dialog questions is easy once you have the framework down.

A dialog questions contains three parts:

1. An observation
2. A contrast or comparison
3. A request for an opinion

Here is an example: "Mr. Jones, I noticed that you have 15 people in your accounting department [Observation]. We have other clients in your industry of similar size who only have 8 to 10 people working in accounting [Comparison]. In what ways do you find the additional people to be helpful? [Opinion]"

Dialog questions that confirm or eliminate problems are good questions for discovering problems. For example, "Mr. Jones, I was reading an article in *Manufacturing Today* about the companies that are moving their production to other countries. When we came in this morning, we noticed you were adding on to your facility. How are you successfully fighting the trend toward moving production offshore?"

Conclusion

Being informed enough to ask the right questions is the professional way to develop a sales relationship. Dialog questions will give you a way to ask good questions in a comfortable manner.

28 Listening: A Key to Uncovering Problems

While good questions are crucial, they are not the only important way to uncover problems. The single most important skill in discovering problems is to listen and pay attention to the answers. Attentive listening is demonstrated in two ways: physically and psychologically. How attentive are you?

How to Show You're Really Listening

Keep the following pointers in mind when meeting with prospects:

- **Face the prospect.** Facing the person tells her you are physically present to talk about the issues directly and openly.
- **Be open.** Have an open smile and convey a sense of receptiveness. Crossing your legs, crossing your arms, and tilting your head back tells the prospect, "I am closed to your thoughts."

- **Lean into the conversation.** Leaning toward your prospect tells your prospect that you are keenly interested in her and the subject matter.

- **Maintain good eye contact.** Looking at the person tells him psychologically that you are on the same level with him.

- **Relax.** Just like a duck swimming along, demonstrate a relaxed demeanor while paddling like crazy to listen carefully, understand, ask follow-up questions, and take good notes. "When selling in teams, assign one person to take notes so the others can focus on the prospect," says David Morgan of LBMC, Nashville, Tennessee. Don't forget that prospects respond to both verbal and nonverbal feedback. It is important to give feedback, even if it's only an "uh-huh" or "I see" from time to time during the conversation.

Listen and Learn

As you listen to your prospect, pay attention to what the prospect says and does not say. In business conversation, the unsaid is often more important than what is said. Your prospect may imply there is no problem or you may infer from what was said there is no problem. When you are in doubt, ask a follow-up question like this, "Sarah, in the situation you just described I expected you might say this, but you didn't. Can you tell me the key reasons that this is not an issue with you?"

A key element in listening is to periodically feed back what the prospect is saying to you. Say something like this: "Jim, this is what I understood was your difficulty: X. Is this accurate?"

Expert listeners can hear with antennae other than their ears. You can listen with your eyes and your heart. Watch for emotional responses from the prospect. This will tell you the issue is more important. A face turning red, a louder voice, or a grin are all signs that you are onto something.

Conclusion

Many professionals have limited training and experience in listening. If this is you, take some courses or read some articles or books on the subject. Commit to improve your listening ability to become better at discovering prospect problems.

29 Researching Your Prospects On The Internet

by Drew Crowder
*Vice President, Waugh & Co., Inc.**

One of the most powerful tools to learn about your prospects' business and industry is the Internet. Before the online information explosion, you were limited to marketing materials and traditional media coverage to get a vague idea of the problems facing your prospects. Now much more and varied information is available to you with the click of a mouse.

The Prospect's Website

The first thing you should do before pursuing or meeting with prospects is review their websites. Few viable businesses today do not have a website, and those that are unwilling to establish a

---

*Drew Crowder, MBA, is Vice President of Waugh & Co. Consulting.

web presence will have to be approached carefully to determine why.

Many websites today go far beyond the "brochure-ware" of the early days of the web. Because of the affordability of the medium, most companies put far more information about the company on the web than they do in printed marketing materials.

Search Engines

Virtually every entity is mentioned on the web somewhere, and more often in a number of different websites. Most popular modern search engines such as Google will have billions upon billions of cross-referenced website entries. This means that if a prospect is mentioned on a web page, even if the page has little to do with that company, that address will show up on most search engines. You might also want to search message board postings (on Google, click the "Group" tab above the search entry box). Here you can find out what customers, suppliers, employees, and others are saying about the company.

Effective use of Internet search engines can be the difference between satisfaction and frustration when searching the web for prospect information. The way to do effective searches is to be specific about the information that you are looking for and use the standard tools of the search engines to focus your search (such as placing a "+" by the words that you want included in the search, "−" in front of words that you want excluded, and quotations around exact phrases that you want to be found; if you're not familiar or comfortable with those conventions, an additional way to narrow your search on Google is to click the "advanced search" link to the right).

Industry-Specific Sites

There is no substitute for industry knowledge when prospecting within an industry niche. Clients want a professional who knows their industry intimately. Many clients will pay a premium to have one. Every industry that has been large enough to support printed periodicals has a comparable web offering with information you can use.

30 Your Business Physical Defines Problems

Just as your physician might ask you to take a series of tests during your annual physical, a solid business professional will diagnose carefully before prescribing. A "business physical" might cover all aspects of a business: environmental, regulatory, tax, financial, personnel, legal, management, and strategy. The Financial Physical process consists of four activities: preparation, the prospect meeting, needs assessment, and presentation. The first three steps are all part of a "discovery" phase of selling.

Preparation

The first activity involves gathering data and preplanning the meeting. Several tools may be used to assist this effort, including the annual financial operations review and other industry and functional checklists. It is imperative that the team understands how the prospect makes money and what the key ingredients are for success. This requires an understanding of the business and the industry.

The Prospect Meeting

The initial meeting should include members of the service team and other specialists who will be involved in the on-site part of the business physical. Because the business physical can take up to three days and requires some intrusiveness, the primary goal of this meeting should be to make the people whose work you will be interrupting believe in the value of the physical. The secondary goal is to create a plan for locating and assembling the information you will need to make meaningful recommendations.

Needs Assessment

The focus of the needs assessment should be on key ingredients for this prospect's success and your ability to provide assistance in achieving it. You need to have a thorough discussion with the prospect about current issues and problems.

Presentation

Once the prospective client's problems and needs have been identified, you are ready to make recommendations. There may or may not be actions that your firm can take to remedy problems you identify. Don't force your services. The generation of goodwill now could reap unforeseen future benefits.

Note: At Waugh & Co. Consulting, we have developed a complete process for conducting a Business Physical. If you'd like a copy, please send your check for $29 to Waugh & Co. Consulting, Box 1208, Brentwood, TN 37024, or call 1-888-797-RAIN (7246)).

Developing Needs

31 Professionals Recommend, They Don't Sell

Consultative professionals create an integrated relationship between their firm and the prospect. Before solving problems, consultants provide a thorough cost-benefit analysis. They create a relationship of trust, support for the prospect's goals, and information sharing that will promote success for the client.

Most of us have a variety of services we want to sell. When we approach a prospect with the notion that we will sell a specific service, we are approaching the situation like a seller of products rather than as a consultative professional. Consultants deal with clients' needs and wants. Consultants think long-term and view the big picture.

Recommend What Benefits the Client

During the discovery phase of selling, you may have uncovered hundreds of problems. Many of the problems you discover will not justify solutions. For example, I worked with a large equipment dealer with millions of dollars invested in inventory. I immediately thought about an inventory control system my firm had expertise in providing. However, I learned that the equipment manufacturer held 90% of the dealer's inventory, shipped directly to the end-user, and kept accurate records for finished goods, shipping, billing, and inventory turnover. My system provided some benefits the manufacturer's system did not. But the cost/benefit of selling my inventory system did not provide a good investment for the client. Had I approached this prospect with this system, he may have listened out of courtesy, but he would have concluded quickly that I was interested in the sale for me, not him.

Sharing your conclusion with the prospect can build credibility. If you say, "John, when I first saw your operation I thought we might have an inventory control system for you that has helped a lot of my other clients. But your current system is working great—it just wouldn't make financial sense for you to change." This lets the prospect know that you have considered this aspect of their business, that you have a product you could try to sell, and that you don't try to sell products that don't make financial sense.

Cost/Benefits for the Client

On the other hand, when you place a quality service in front of a client that solves a costly problem, sometimes you don't have to ask for the sale. The client asks you.

The real key to discovering needs is to understand the value of solving a problem. If a problem can be solved for 10% of the cost, it is likely a need. If a problem is causing other problems, which in their totality is huge, fixing the root problem may very well represent a need.

Conclusion

The consultative professional thinks past the services sale to the needs of the client and to the long-term relationship.

32 Take Your Problem Questions Deeper

Your analyses of prospects' and clients' businesses should focus on the problems that need solving. By asking a series of questions designed to size up the problem, its severity, and its impact on other costs or problems, you are able to get the prospect to tell you if this is a need. A need is a problem that is cost justified to fix. Cost can be justified in dollars or in hassle.

Costing Problems

Some novice professionals may be uncomfortable asking problem questions. However, taking your problem questions deeper in order to get your prospect to project the effect of problems on other problems and opportunities, is a powerful way to uncover needs. For example, you might discover that total accounts receivable are averaging 65 days before collection. You have also confirmed that management perceives this as a problem. You could ask, "What does it cost you annually for the working capital for accounts over 30 days old?" Or, you could go on, "What does it cost you, in terms of accounting department staff and mailing and telephoning, to collect accounts once they exceed 30 days old?"

When your prospects say something themselves, they believe it more than they do if you say it. You could certainly say, "You have $560,000 tied up in accounts over 30 days, so you stand to lose $140,000 from the sales you have made. And your working capital line is at 5% per year. So your working capital costs you over $28,000. You have one full-time person sending letters, making calls, and responding to requests for back-up, etc. This person costs you $50,000 per year in salary, benefits, office space, training, and supervision." But by saying all this, you could be putting your prospect in a defensive position. If you are able to get your prospects to say this, then they will not be as defensive and will be more likely to recognize that they have a need.

Conclusion

When your prospects answer your questions, they will remember what they said more than they will remember what you said. This process is very helpful in preparing your prospects to tell other people in their organizations about the issues. When you can prepare your prospect for internal selling, you are impacting the sale at many levels in the business.

33 Benchmarking to Discover Needs

Top companies compare themselves to leaders not just in their industries, but in any process they are interested in. For instance, a company might benchmark its customer service against Nordstrom, even though it's not a department store. Same-industry benchmarking gives you an idea of the standards you are competing with in your type of business. Process-oriented benchmarking against other industries gives you a standard for what is possible, plus fresh ideas.

A Benchmarking Tool for Prospects and Clients

One of the most helpful tools you can use to help prospects develop and define their needs is a benchmarking tool. A benchmarking tool allows you to compare information about your prospect against standards. When your prospect's data vary from the standard, this provides you an opportunity for creating a dialog around the issue.

Which benchmarking tool is the right tool for you? One of the leading benchmarking sources is a Robert Morris Associates (RMA) book that gives industry averages for things like sales per square foot, average gross, average profit margins, and so on. Many banks use the RMA data for comparison purposes when making decisions about loans. The comparisons quickly highlight how businesses are doing or when projections are unrealistic.

Some professional firms have developed their own benchmarking data because they have many clients in a particular industry. For example, PricewaterhouseCoopers has developed a benchmarking tool they call advanced middle market business intelligence tool—or AMMBIT. This PwC tool was developed from business data input by many CPAs from many firms.

Sageworks has an industry comparison program that captures data from a variety of sources. The unique aspect of the Sageworks program is that it provides a written analysis of the benchmarked data for you to provide your client.

Develop Your Own Benchmarking Tool

You could devise a custom tool that applied across industries for your clients. It could be as simple as a checklist asking if they had a business succession plan, a will, audited financials, a disaster contingency plan, adequate financial reserves, a line of credit, or other areas in which you specialize. It could also go into more depth in one area.

Conclusion

The best benchmarking tools give an "objective" picture of how a business compares to others. It could also use customer perceptions or wants as standards. For instance, clients tell us that they judge accountants, attorneys, and other professionals by how well they are treated in little interactions. They are more impressed by how fast their calls are returned than by professional certifications and similar measures of technical competence. Yet most firms don't have standards for returning phone calls or keeping in touch with clients when not doing work for them.

34 Differentiate Your Service

A key to uncovering prospect needs is to clearly differentiate you and your firm's services from other similar providers in your marketplace. There are mega-firms, tiny firms, and all kinds of firms in between. There are specialty firms, boutique firms, and department store firms (one-stop shops). When you clearly differentiate your firm by identifying the best clients and the needs you can best help with, you increase the potential for serving that need early in the relationship.

An Example

Some firms differentiate along industry lines or by type of client. Others develop deep expertise in a service line. For instance, the Sunnyvale, California, law firm Day Casebeer Madrid & Batchelder, LLP focuses their 30-lawyer operation on intellectual property litigation for a few large clients. Crowe Chizek, LLP has grown rapidly over the past 15 years by focusing on consulting businesses, community banks, auto dealers, and manufacturing.

You can have more than one speciality, but each client is only interested in your ability to uniquely serve their needs. This means that, ultimately, your goal is to build a relationship with the client that can't be duplicated. This relationship occurs on two dimensions. First, the principles of one-to-one marketing say for you to invest in customizing your services for each client. When clients invest in "educating" you on how to customize your services for them, they will not want to spend the time developing other service providers.

Second, the ultimate differentiation that no one else can match is YOU. You are a unique individual. Rather than suppressing your individuality to achieve some sort of neutral "professionalism," you should be both professional and individual. Many professionals make the mistake of thinking that clients hire them for their expertise, as if they were plug-in modules with a particular skill. If that were the case, you would be a commodity. You must be an individual. When clients feel comfortable and taken care of by you as a person, they won't want to risk going elsewhere.

Conclusion

You need to understand how to differentiate yourself and your business. First, know your speciality and your services inside and out. Being able to articulate your expertise is impressive to clients and prospects. Second, stress that the key differentiator in working with you is you. No matter how big the client firm, people always work with people. And they decide to engage you based on the differences they believe are important. You are the most important differentiator.

EIGHT

The "R" Word....

35 Creating Wants

Quick, write down something tangible you need. Now write down something tangible you want. Put a price tag next to each item. What you generally will learn is that most people's wants are much more expensive than their needs. Your clients are the same way.

If you focus on analyzing needs, you have missed the most important element of selling: emotion. People decide to do things emotionally and then justify it with logic, not the other way around. Once you have discovered problems, you must ferret out the ones the prospect *wants* to solve. You are going to have much more success if you focus on his want rather than your logical analysis.

How to Create Wants

How do you create wants? You must work with the prospect in a consulting manner to help her define the problems and needs, then to clarify the emotional and financial benefits available from solving the problems. A business owner with a net worth of $5 million might want to control his business and wealth long after he is gone. He might want to pay the minimum in taxes and preserve the most for his heirs. Another prospect, with the same financial profile, may not want to talk about his demise or mortality. He may want to maximize his results while living, but not face dying. Trying to force estate or succession planning on prospect number two will create major resistance.

The questions you ask will get the prospect to tell you what he wants from your service and how he sees it benefiting him or his business. Call these questions "benefit questions." For example, ask, "How would it help you if we worked with you to provide some succession ideas for your company?"

You can ask about the benefits and then ask further questions about the implied benefits your prospect will receive from the solutions. For example, "If you had things planned out, how would that help your spouse? Or your children? Or your business partner?"

Conclusion

When the prospect says to you, "I want this," or he says, "I need this" you are getting at the wants. It takes an explicit response from your prospect for you to satisfy his wants. That makes the sale.

36 Listening Is Key to Creating Wants

Almost every book on selling has a chapter on asking questions. Marketing and sales trainers encourage you to ask, "Open-ended questions." In many cases, these books and trainers miss the main point: to encourage your client to tell you what's on her mind. You do not benefit from the question, but from the answer.

I believe listening is suspending one's own judgments to really hear what someone else is saying. Listening is 10 times more important than talking.

Great Listening = Great Relationships

In his book *The Seven Habits of Highly Effective People*, Steven Covey writes, "If I were to summarize the single most important principle in the field of interpersonal relationships, listening is the key." Listening is vital to building trusting relationships. Trusting relationships are fundamental to marketing your firm's services. Of the four ways we communicate, listening skills are rarely taught in formal education. In colleges and CPE programs, you will find many courses on reading, writing, and speaking, but few on listening.

Good listening is the most powerful communication device to build trust with other people. When you listen and understand, your client responds by naming you his "most trusted business adviser." Covey explains five levels of listening: ignoring, pretending, selective, attentive, and empathic. Ignoring and pretending will ruin relationships. Selective listeners miss key points. The highest form, empathic listening, is a way to understand emotions and words. I want to help you deal with attentive listening, a higher level of listening to which we can all aspire.

Conclusion

Even great sellers have had difficulty learning to listen. One of the top rainmakers in the country, Terry Orr, partner with Belew Averitt, LLP in Dallas, said, "I had been working with clients for years and suddenly it dawned on me, I needed to learn how to listen better. To help clients with their deepest problems requires my understanding first. When I understand completely, only then can I be a true adviser."

37 Keys to Better Listening for Wants

As already mentioned, listening is more important than asking questions, and asking questions is more important than talking. Yet there is almost no training in listening for professionals. Here are three keys to help improve your ability to listen.

Listen Attentively

Picture this. As you arrive home, your child begins to tell you about an event that took place that day. You continue to change clothes, set the table for dinner, and so forth while your child continues with his important tale. Finally, exasperated, your child stops you, grabs you by the face, looks into your eyes and with total honesty says, "Please look at me when I'm talking to you!"

This scenario presents the perfect example of two keys to attentive listening: showing attention in behavior and in eye contact. What message were you sending the child by working on other tasks and not maintaining eye contact? Have you ever met with someone while they opened their mail? Not maintaining attention and eye contact is perceived as ignoring. And, ignoring is insulting.

Do you ever do this? When you are talking with someone on the phone, do you shuffle papers, type, or play video games? The other party knows that you aren't listening, even though you may not be visible. (For instance, they can often hear the computer clicking.) What about when a staff member or assistant comes into your office. Do you keep working on what you are doing, or do you suspend what you are doing and make eye contact with your associate? Remember, if your associate feels ignored, he is insulted.

Pause before Replying

Some people speak immediately because they are just waiting for their turn to speak, and are not really listening. Others respond fast because they think fast. In either case, it is not flattering to the speaker. Taking a second or two before you reply to the other person indicates that you are preparing a thoughtful response. This is a learned technique.

Prepare Good Questions

One of the best ways to involve your prospect is to ask good questions, and then carefully listen to the answers.

In preparing for a prospect meeting, it is crucial to develop your questions in advance. You should have some key questions that you can use in many situations. Others will be customized for each prospect. Preparing written questions enables you to focus on listening. If your mind is busy constructing your next question, you may miss the deep message your client is articulating.

38 Active Listening

A ctive listening means showing the person who is speaking to you that he or she has your full attention.

Remove Distractions

In order to listen, you should remove as many distractions as possible. Cut off your cell phone or computer screen. Show that you are not distracted.

Take Notes

Have a notepad or white board available. Taking notes shows you are actively listening. Try boiling down each point into a few words that capture the thought. Writing it so the prospect can see will let her know you have it.

Have you ever had someone finish your sentences before you do? It comes from either impatience or a powerful urge to get our thoughts out of our head, lest we forget them. Rather than jump on someone else's train of thought, it is better to jot your thought down. That way you won't lose your thought either and you can focus on active listening.

Restate and Prompt

Periodically restate what your client is saying as you are capturing the words. Ask for explanation and clarification. A good question to have available at all times is, "How do you mean?" Asking this question will encourage the client to talk at a deeper level.

Acknowledge that You're Listening

Active listening includes responding so your client knows you are listening. Phrases like, "I see," "uh huh," or "that's interesting" all let the other person know you are in tune. Be careful. Using these inappropriately shows your client that you are pretending to listen. Pretending is one of the quickest ways to break trust with people.

Conclusion

When talking with another person, most people have a limited capacity to remember things. If your client has five things he wants to talk to you about, let him talk through them once before you begin probing any of the issues. Otherwise, the memory capacity may become overloaded and you may miss "The Key Issue." Often "The Key Issue," that one major, emotional problem your client has, will not come out as the first item.

39 Stimulate Wants with Perceived Value

Whenever clients work with professionals, they want the perception that they are getting more than compliance knowledge. Business clients want you to understand them. Understanding is the root of almost every person's desires. When you take industry training, attend industry conferences, and read industry journals, you are working to understand the client and his industry. But it is critical not just to know their industries, but that your clients and prospects *know* that you know. You may develop deep expertise, but if the prospect doesn't perceive your expertise, he won't be affected.

The most successful and profitable firms help their people relate to *clients'* perceptions of value. Yet it is likely that you and your clients have differing views on the value of your services.

Show You're on Their Side

Clients and prospects want an advocate. When a prospect meets with an attorney, an accountant, or consultant, he wants the professional to be on his side before telling the prospect all the things that are wrong. Clients want proactive advocates as well. Recommending creative ideas and informing clients and prospects of pending legislation or conditions that might help or hurt business is a good way to be proactive in delivering ideas.

When asked, many professionals rate the value of their work in terms of the hours they have worked, the accuracy of their work, and the compliance of the work to the appropriate standards.

On the other hand, what your clients see as value is completely different. They're probably not capable of judging the technical quality of your work. Instead, clients of professional firms see perceived value in terms of trust, response time, and the quality of the relationship.

Conclusion

What are you doing to improve *your prospect's perceptions* of your value? A well-managed firm increases a client's confidence and comfort. Trust and relationships are key. You can build these by implementing a policy to improve your response time, and by increasing the friendliness to, and personal treatment of, each client.

40 Doing the "Needs to Wants" Two-Step

*by Charles Flood**

Step One: Knowing the "Why" and the "How" Is What You Are Trained to Do

Before you start any engagement, ask yourself, "Why did they really come to me?" Exposing the client's "why" behind your solution is how you build a client's transactional needs into high-impact wants.

There is a difference between preparing an audit, and preparing that same audit with a strategic planning offer letter attached based on an analysis of the audit results for the client. The audit shows where the business is today, while the letter offers a vision for the future. It highlights the needs of the com-

*Charles Flood is a consultant for The Rainmaker Academy.

pany for the management team, and it helps the client focus on their wants and creates an opportunity to realize a greater return on your investment of wisdom and time.

Management guru Steven Covey tells us to "begin with the end in mind." We want our clients to understand what it is they really want when they come to us with a "simple need." Remember: your clients want you to help them meet their needs. They come prepared to tell you what they want. Are you really listening to your clients?

Step Two: Add Two Emotionally Driven Ego Questions

Asking "Why do you want this?" or "What is the worst that can happen if you don't do this?" help the client to build a deeper personal understanding of the value you bring to the process.

Conclusion

Understanding the prospects' or clients' needs and wants helps them better understand the value of your services. When you give your client what they really want, they will want more in the future. In the end, isn't this what we want, too?

Building Like and Trust

41 Creating a Brand Stimulates Trust

Question: What is branding?

1. That thing they burn into cows
2. A logo
3. A slogan
4. I don't really know, but I'll look like an idiot if I admit it.

Of course, the term "brand" historically referred to searing the hide of one rancher's cattle with his distinctive mark so that it couldn't be confused with anyone else's.

Many firm owners and marketing professionals get carried away with the concept of branding. Most branding efforts end with wasted dollars and little results. One managing partner said he'd "thrown $100,000 down that rat hole."

Branding is a way of "packaging" a professional firm. It should position you uniquely in people's minds. Branding should not only attract new clients, but reinforce your existing clients' buying decisions.

Firm Consistency

The point, of course, is that if you work hard to make your service that much better than everyone else's, you want to make sure that the differentiation isn't lost on your prospective buyers. In fact, you want to go out of your way to make sure they don't miss it.

The problem in branding your firm is the lack of consistency from one partner to another. The reason that McDonald's has one of the most successful brands is not because of the gourmet quality of their food. It is because of the consistency of the customer experience worldwide. The potential customer believes that each McDonald's experience will be the same.

The same cannot be said of a firm. Each partner or associate is a separate experience in many firms.

Branding Is Personal

The fundamental reasons why brands work are twofold: (1) client trust and (2) service consistency.

In his book *Trust in The Balance,* Robert Bruce Shaw says that trust requires integrity, *concern,* and results. From the client's point of view, a professional firm can have the highest integrity and achieve excellent results. But without *concern* you will be unsuccessful in establishing trust. That's the personal side of branding.

Conclusion

When your firm is consistent across partners, you are more easily able to build like and trust. Trust and consistency build a brand.

42 Like Me, Like My Team

One of the best ways to get people to like you is to first get them to enjoy dealing with your team.

The Most Important Marketer in Your Firm

A vital link in your team is your receptionist. It's true. Did you know that callers talk with your receptionist two to three times more frequently than they talk with you? Every time your phone rings, your business is on the line.

A frugal-minded office often concludes that the receptionist has spare time when not answering the phone. So the receptionist is assigned administrative filler work. That way, when a prospect calls or comes into the office, often the receptionist will be too busy to help him. This happened to me recently. I walked into a reception area and the receptionist did not acknowledge me for several minutes because she was too busy entering data into a spreadsheet.

Or we decide that the newest member of our administrative staff should handle the phone. Seems logical, doesn't it? Assign the person with the least knowledge of our firm the job with the most contact with our prospects!

Then there is the question of training. I am sure the ones I've talked to in the past six weeks had no instruction into what to say when answering calls. Here are some quotes I've heard recently from receptionists from professionals' offices: At 2:30 P.M., "He's not come in yet, I'll put you to his voice mail." CLICK. "He's gone for the day, please call back tomorrow. . . ." "Are you with a company?" "Accounting offices! . . ." "Does he know you? . . ." "Does he know what you're calling about?"

Conclusion

Many firms have "trained" their number one marketing agent to *repel* business rather than attract it. The frightening aspect is that many firms are spending tens of thousands of dollars and countless hours on marketing programs to attract prospects while they let a low-paid receptionist cost them business.

You can make your receptionist a marketing asset rather than a liability with a little creative thought at no expense.

Note: Appendix C provides a sample 30-day training program for your new receptionist.

43 Table Manners Sell or Repel

People form an impression of your professionalism based on your table manners.

Recently, I enjoyed a lunch with several younger professionals. One of them told me he had recently dined with a partner and a prospective client. He reported that, "After the dinner, my partner suggested that, before entertaining clients again, I improve my table manners."

If you define marketing as communication, and intend to build relationships with prospects and clients, then good entertaining skills are essential to a good marketing program. Let's cover a few of the basics for a successful power lunch.

Treat Your Guests with Respect

Open doors for your guests and encourage them to precede you to the table. Allow your guest to be seated first, in the most preferred seats. If there is a good view, encourage the guest to face that direction. Give your undivided attention to your guests. Always allow your guest to go first: ordering drinks or the meal, taking the first sip or bite, and ordering coffee or desert.

The host's responsibility is to carry a convivial conversation. You may be intimidated, but if you sit through your meal without joining in the conversation, you are communicating to your guest that you are not interested.

Order Foods that Are Easy to Eat

Avoid any foods that cannot be controlled easily. If you aren't skilled at twirling pasta, don't order it; it will be too messy. Shellfish that requires squeezing and digging, ribs, corn on the cob, and fried chicken are all difficult to eat daintily. Tear your roll gently; don't saw it with a knife.

Never talk with food in your mouth (so take small bites so you can easily enter conversations). When you feel that bit of food between your teeth, swish it out silently and unobtrusively. Only cut and take one bite of food at a time.

Blot lipstick so it does not appear on glasses. And never place your napkin in the middle of a dirty plate. Sit up straight in your chair. Don't hover or slump over your plate or lean your chair back on two legs. Keep elbows off the table.

What About Drinks, Appetizers, and Dessert?

Always offer these to your guests, and if they order one, order something yourself. Never let them eat a course alone. Appetizers or dessert should not be shared, unless your guest asks to. Then, ask the server to split it for you.

Conclusion

Table manners may seem too basic to cover. But many people form impressions of you from simple things. So brush up on your etiquette and table manners for better results. If you feel your staff would benefit, arrange a catered lunch and hire an etiquette trainer to teach the basics. When people are confident of their manners, they can focus their attention on the client rather than worrying about what they might be doing wrong.

44 When Your Prospect Visits

Imagine that you are visiting a professional firm for the first time.

You tell yourself that this is going to be the year when you really hold the line on fees. Old Reliable, LLP has been the firm you've hired for 10 years now, and for the most part, you guess they are doing a good job. However, your banker has made an appointment for you with Steve Bennett at Likem & Trustem whom he recommends highly.

You've assembled all of the materials that you think you need for your 9:00 A.M. meeting with Steve at Likem & Trustem's offices. The materials checklist Steve sent you was really helpful and you have everything that the list indicated you needed.

By the time you arrive, it's 8:50 A.M. You're actually early for your appointment (no thanks to the weather) and the directions that Steve emailed to you yesterday sure helped. Come to think of it, you hadn't asked for the directions, Steve had just called to confirm the appointment and offered to send the map.

First Impressions: Feeling Welcome

As you step off of the elevator, you find yourself in a comfortable reception area that looks a lot like a large living room. The receptionist is currently on the phone, but another person comes out from around the counter and is walking toward you. "Good morning, Mr. Smith," she says with a smile, " I'm Susan Jones, the Director of First Impressions here. May I take your coat?"

"Can I get you something to drink? We have both regular and decaffeinated coffee (so that's what you smell!) or tea, bottled water, and soft drinks."

"Good morning, Mr. Smith," the receptionist says as she hangs up the phone, "I'll let Mr. Bennett know that you're here." You notice that there are several issues of today's *Wall Street Journal, USA Today,* and some materials on Likem & Trustem. You dig into an interesting article.

As you wait for your 9 A.M. appointment, you can't quite keep yourself from observing what is going on around you. Visitors are called by name, coats disappear onto sturdy hangers, refreshments are served, and soft music continues to play in the background.

About halfway through your article, Steve comes out to greet you. As he leads you back toward the conference rooms, Susan asks you if you were able to finish the article you were reading. She tells you that on your way out, she'll have a copy of it waiting to take with you.

Conclusion

The next time you walk into your office, come in as if you were a prospect. What image is your receptionist presenting? Your reception area? What have you done to prepare visitors ahead of time to have a positive experience? If you're not satisfied with the answers, think about inexpensive ways of improving the situation.

45 Active Professionals Give Back

Professionals who give back to their communities are well liked by all business people. You are often called upon to donate time and money to not-for-profit (NFP) organizations. This is a good thing, but as the joke goes, "Not-for-profits means not-for-profit for the service provider, too."

I do not want to limit or discourage your participation and support for religious, civic, and social causes, but I can help you turn your *not-for-profit* engagements into *for-profit* investments.

Stop Discounting Your Fees

Rather than discounting your fees, make a contribution to your client that equals the discount you have been taking. When you contribute to the NFP, you will appear on the contributors list, and you may be allowed to present your check to the board. Discounting makes you appear to be a low bidder (cheap fees), whereas making a contribution tells the client you are a benefactor. There is a huge difference in the perception by the governing board and the people they refer to you.

Support Your Partners' and Staff's Activities

When you have staff members involved in charitable organizations, support their activities with firm donations or services. Too often, professionals spread their support among too many organizations. Contributing $100 to 10 organizations will not be as effective for you as $1,000 to one group. Backing a firm member will create even more impact.

Offer Your Office for Meetings

Making your office available costs you nothing and can benefit you in big ways. When board members of an NFP visit your offices, they may think about accounting or tax matters. Getting them on your turf will encourage them to talk to you about their business or personal needs.

Get to Know the Board Members

Usually the board members of NFPs are movers and shakers in your community. Take them to lunch or breakfast and get to know them. When you share a common interest in an NFP's mission, you have a theme for your visits. These board members can be valuable sources of referrals and new business.

Conclusion

Appearing to use an NFP agency for selling new business is not a good image to convey. When you are getting to know the board members, refrain from talking about your services until someone asks. On the other hand, don't take this word of caution so seriously that you use it as an excuse not to get to know each board member. Tom Hopkins says, "Sell like a lion, but act like a lamb."

If you are going to serve on an NFP's board or donate fees to their cause, you should make it your marketing mission to develop relationships with everyone.

TEN

Demonstrating Capabilities

46 Demonstrating Your Capabilities Correctly

In every commercial relationship, there is an appropriate time to demonstrate your capabilities to solve the problems of a prospect. Demonstrating your capabilities too soon will create the perception that your solutions are not client centric. Clients who do not believe you are addressing *their* concerns will not be positively impacted with your recommendations.

At the right time, written and oral proposals can be helpful selling tools. If you want your demonstration of capabilities to be competitive, keep in mind the following guidelines:

Focus on the Benefits the Client Will Receive from You

You must articulate your in-depth understanding of the client's problems, needs, and wants. Your ability to prioritize these issues will clearly set you apart from many of your competitors. Benefits are only derived from explicit needs (wants), so you must ensure that your client's interests are foremost. In his book, *Strategic Proposals,* Bob Kantin says that clients want two types of benefits: financial (quantitative) and nonfinancial (qualitative). Make sure you include elements of both in your proposals.

Include Recommendations for Implementation

Specific approaches for services, products, approaches, or designs will be more convincing than generalities. You must tailor the specific approaches to assure the prospect he will receive the benefits you have promised. Show a step-by-step approach for action. Clearly state what you will do, what your client will do, and what happens if either party needs help doing his job.

Show Evidence of Your Past Successes

Testimonials or descriptions of past assignments can be powerful evidence that you can handle the client's needs. Mentioning your experience with similar clients in the same industry is helpful. Discussing your access to other resources, such as banks or international alliances, can be helpful if you cannot help with the specific benefits the prospect wants.

Give Convincing Reasons Why the Prospect Should Choose You

Compare and contrast your firm with your competitors to show how you are uniquely suited to serve this client. While you shouldn't speak negatively about your competitor, you can draw fair comparisons. For example, you could say, "That firm has a great reputation in working with governmental agencies, but their experience with sophisticated manufacturers is limited. You do want a firm you won't have to train, don't you?"

Conclusion

Using a written proposal document, PowerPoint slides, and other visual aids can be helpful in making successful presentations. However, you must not make the visual aids the presentation. Many successful sales presentations are made on a legal pad. Keep this in mind, so that your sales aids support the points you make, not replace you.

47 Tell a Story, Draw a Picture

A picture is worth a thousand words. You may not be much of an artist, but everyone can tell stories that sketch powerful word-pictures in the mind of a prospect. A good story can punch up your presentation of capabilities more than any fancy brochure.

Telling stories helps sell intangible services. With a tangible product, prospects can see it, touch it, and try it out. With intangible services, there is nothing to touch, so craft a carefully worded picture to entice your prospect.

Case Studies Sell

Telling the right story in the right situation can be a powerful sales tool that demonstrates your capabilities to deliver quantitative and qualitative benefits. Using stories is a form of persuasion. Relating a story is a more compelling way to make your point, rather than just stating some facts. Stories appeal to the emotions and can give you a decisive edge in the competitive game of demonstrating your capabilities.

Dr. Paul Homoly, an author, coach, and storyteller, says that the most compelling reason for people to engage your professional firm is other people who found that your solution solved their problems. After all, what is a service firm? In one way, it's the success stories of its clients.

How to Construct Stories

Dr. Homoly says the best way to tell stories is to combine them with business objectives. Homoly trademarked a phrase, Storyselling, to describe the concept that includes narratives, color-ful comparisons, metaphors, and similes to help clients under-stand, believe, and remember what you say—to actually feel your message.

Suppose a prospect asks why your service costs more than others. Instead of launching into a spiel heavy on numbers, cre-ate a story:

1. Think of a client who had the same objection, but is now a happy client.
2. Tell your prospect about the client.
3. Recount the specifics.
4. Describe the client's current situation.
5. Explain the lesson the client learned.
6. Transfer the lesson to the present situation.

To have the greatest impact, your stories should include some personal experience. One of the best resources you can use on the subject of Storyselling is Scott West's *Storyselling for Financial Advisors*.

Conclusion

To have the best impact when demonstrating capabilities, tell a story to illustrate how your new client will enjoy the benefits of working with you. By telling a story, you cover the qualitative as well as the quantitative reasons for hiring you.

48 Demonstrate Your Value

When demonstrating your capabilities, it is crucial to illustrate the value of your services compared with your potential competitors. Illustrating value will create less price resistance when the time comes to hire you.

Prospects want a superior service, one that comes with added benefits such as strong technology and staff training. They want assurance that their delivery schedules will be met and that if they have a problem, you will be there for them.

Many prospects want a professional firm that can provide a variety of services, rather than just one specialized service. This is called a business relationship. To the extent your firm focuses on building relationships by solving a variety of business problems, you should demonstrate that you can provide value by developing long-term relationships. Using client testimonials is a good way to illustrate the value clients have received from your services.

Stay Away from Feature Language

The key ingredient to demonstrating value is to ensure that your language is benefit-oriented rather than feature-oriented. Many professionals talk in terms of the features provided by their firms. Size of firm, number of partners, services provided, and location of offices are all features of your firm. I have heard many a boring partner attempt to wax eloquent about the size and scope of his firm. Features are of interest to the seller and of very little interest to the buyer.

Advantages Are an Improvement

Each feature of your firm has an advantage. For example one could say, "We have 12 partners, which gives us the ability to provide our clients with a diversity of experience and specialty." Advantages are slightly more powerful than feature language because you are talking possible benefits. So long as the prospect is interested in "a diversity of experience and specialty" you might hit a hot button. Or you might not.

Benefits Express Value in the Prospect's Terms

Demonstrating the quality you build into your service is crucial to clients' understanding the difference in your value compared with that of your competitors. However, make certain that the prospect cares about quality level. If the prospect asks about how your associates are trained, you can talk about the quality education each of them has, and about your professional training programs. This is benefit-oriented.

Conclusion

When you sell value rather than features or services, prospects better understand what they are buying.

49 Demonstrate Capabilities with Passion

When demonstrating your firm's capabilities, it is important to feel and demonstrate the passion you feel about delivering services. For instance, in a survey performed by Huthwaite a few years ago, clients of accounting firms indicated that while the candor and competence of their professional was high, less than 35% thought their accountant *really cared about them.* When you are passionate, clients believe that you care.

Are you passionate about *delivering* technically correct documents, or are you passionate about *helping* clients make better business decisions, develop win-win relationships with their customers, obtain financing, and use their core competencies? If you are passionate about delivering products, then your branding and strategic positioning will take one approach. However, if you are passionate about helping, your message will be completely different.

When You Sell Relationships

Let's take a common example: You have decided that your best clients want relationships that are not built on price or upon you having the latest "doodad" connected with your technical services. A relationship means that the clients want you to become an expert in their businesses, help create custom solutions to their problems, and serve as a valuable extension of their decision-making team. You need to be passionate about what your best clients want year round. Or are you too busy doing technical work much of the year?

If you are going to develop a successful capabilities demonstration, you must connect what your best clients want with what you provide, with passion.

Conclusion

Even commodities can be demonstrated with passion when you connect with an interested customer. One of the hottest selling and most profitable items is bottled water, a commodity that is available almost for free. So don't tell me, "Our products have become such commodities, we can't demonstrate with passion." If you are serving a passionate client base with a passionate service team, you can demonstrate with passion. And passion is contagious—your clients will be passionate about you, too.

50 Bundling Your Services

Clients want professionals who recognize all their needs and wants.

We have learned that firms that adopt a clear marketing strategy when they add each new service are those that succeed while others languish. The number one strategy of a successful marketing effort is to use bundling to add new services onto old ones. Bundling is simply the process of offering two or more services together. Bundling services often requires a new name for a traditional service.

An Example

Let's look at products for a moment as examples of bundling. Often, bundled products are complimentary in nature: toothbrush and toothpaste, computer and software. However, this is not always the case. Multiproduct bundling combines products that satisfy different needs for the consumer, for example, Hasbro Play-Doh bundled with Lucky Charm cereal. While some forms of product bundling are promotional in nature and have a short life span, other forms of bundling can develop into long-term, sustainable "new" products. Automobile bundling takes place when the new car dealer offers you financing, service, and insurance services as part of the purchase. Bundling takes place from your credit card company when travel, credit, insurance, and many other services are included. Bundling can also take place when you bundle your services with another provider. Law firms routinely bundle their tax services with an accounting firm.

The Advantages of Bundling

Bundling services can provide your firm a strong competitive advantage in the market place. It can dramatically improve your marketing return on investment. And because bundling should be client-driven, your selling process is more productive.

In marketing circles, bundling is categorized by two different theories: the Price Discrimination Theory and the Leverage Theory. Originally, the Price Discrimination Theory saw bundling as a method used by a monopolistic firm to engage in price discrimination. Today, however, bundling can be seen as an optimal selling strategy for a multiservices firm with access to a client. In contrast, the Leverage Theory views bundling as an instrument enabling a firm with some monopoly power in one market to use the leverage provided by this power to achieve sales in, and thereby monopolize, a second market.

Conclusion

In their book *Rethinking the Sales Force,* authors Neil Rackham and John DeVincentis classify customers into three different categories: intrinsic value (commodity buyers), extrinsic value (brand and image buyers), and strategic value buyers. Bundling services will enable you to move clients from commodity buyers to extrinsic value buyers, and others who are extrinsic buyers to strategic buyers. Bundling services can dramatically improve your revenue yield per person or per hour.

51 Improving Your Presentation Versatility

Novice professionals develop only one method for presenting because it is the method they are most comfortable using. However, consider this question: To persuade a buyer, should you use a method of communication that *he* is most comfortable hearing or should you use a method *you* are most comfortable using?

You will be most effective using a method with which both you and the buyer are comfortable. If you are left-brained, linear thinking, and logical, you will have difficulty with raucous, table pounding, emotional presentations. But it can be very effective to be more versatile with your presentation styles.

Different people respond differently to the same demonstration. The following five approaches can be combined to match your style with the styles of your prospects.

Enthusiastic

Enthusiasm is a powerful form of influence because it tends to be contagious. Your prospects get excited when you infect them with your enthusiasm. How many times have you felt low and had someone inject a bubbling personality into your day? It lifted your spirits, didn't it? Prospects are more inclined to buy when they are in a good mood. Enthusiasm is effective with most people.

Congruency

Sending a consistent message is best achieved when your words, tempo, gestures, and body language send the same message. When you describe your firm's aggressive approach to client service, do you talk in a matter-of-fact fashion or do you lean into the conversation? When you verbally speak "yes," so should your body language.

Logic

If your client is the logical, pragmatic type, you will be most effective talking about practical issues. Talk about cost effectiveness, delivery schedules, and sequential implementation. Make your points so they follow a logical train of thought that satisfies your prospect's needs and wants.

Language

When talking, do you use words that have a negative or positive connotation? For example, when describing your competitors you might want to describe them as a cheap alternative. But, when describing your services you would say, "we pride ourselves in being cost effective." Words and phrases have the ability to depress or excite your prospect. Stay away from negative words like busy, cost, problems, objections, and no. Use power words like opportunity, investment, challenges, concerns, and yes.

Word Pictures

Most people think in pictures. The most effective presenters use many word pictures to convey and color meaning. For example, when describing your responsiveness, you could say, "faster than a speeding bullet." This connotes your speed with a word picture. The more you can use illustrations so that your prospect can draw a picture in his mind, the more effective a presenter you will be.

Handling Objections

52 What Is Your Attitude toward Objections?

An objection is anything the prospect says or does that presents an obstacle to the smooth completion of the sale. Objections are a normal and natural part of almost every conversation, not just in sales situations. People just seem to enjoy objecting, no matter what the subject of the conversation might be.

Having seen deception, cover-ups, and dishonesty among the great and near-great, people do not readily accept what somebody says at face value anymore, especially if the person talking is a virtual stranger. Purchases are more often than not made from a person or a company that is somewhat unknown. A purchasing decision, therefore, feels like a risk. To ease the fear of risk, people object or ask questions in hopes of getting answers that will convince them that the buying decision is in their best interest.

Objections Show Interest

Professionals look positively at the objections prospects offer. Objections move prospects nearer to the close and reveal what they are thinking. Sellers who are never forced to deal with objections are just order takers.

Your success in selling depends on how you deal with objections. View objections as opportunities to rise to your highest professional level, not as insurmountable obstacles that you will inevitably fail to climb. An objection often reveals the key to a successful sale.

If the prospect has been properly qualified as a class "A" prospect, objections are really buying signals. Offering an objection is another way for the prospect to say, "Here are my conditions for buying," or "I want to buy as soon as you give me a few more facts or reassure me that buying is the smart thing to do." Because an objection is a request for more information or for reassurance, it should be viewed as an opportunity and not as a problem.

Welcome Objections

The truly serious problem is the prospect who never raises an objection or asks a questions. Then you have no way to discover when to close or what is blocking a buying decision. *Welcome all objections.* They are the verbal and nonverbal signs of sales resistance that give you the chance to discover what the prospect is thinking. They are leverage for closing the sale.

Conclusion

Objections actually indicate that the prospect is interested in your proposal. Statistics show that successful sales presentations, those that end in a sale, have 58% more objections than those presentations that are unsuccessful. Most qualified prospects raise no objections to a proposal in which they have no interest. They just wait and say no.

53 Why Prospects Object

Professionals suggest that the sale does not begin until the prospect raises an objection. Objections may be real and logical, or purely psychological.

Psychological Reasons for Objections

Much sales resistance is largely psychological:

- Dislike of making a decision
- Reluctance to give up something familiar
- Difficulty of changing habits or procedures
- Unpleasant associations with a particular company or sales representative
- Resistance to domination (symbolized by accepting the seller's recommendations)
- Perceived threat to the self-image
- Fear of the unknown

Psychological resistance must be handled through anticipation and preparation ahead of time.

Logical Objections

Consider the possibility that the objection arises from one of these three logical sources:

- **A portion of the presentation was misunderstood.** Usually the prospect lacks knowledge about the product itself, the seller, or the company. The seller must accept responsibility for this type of objection and learn to do a better job of relating benefits to the prospect's needs.

- **The prospect is not convinced.** Professional selling is believing something yourself and convincing others. If the prospect is not convinced, the seller has produced too little evidence to establish credibility in the prospect's mind. As a result, the prospect hesitates to buy. Objections are often an attempt to gain more evidence to support the seller's buying recommendations. Evidence is justification for the emotional decision the prospect is struggling to make.

- **The prospect has an underlying hidden reason to object.** Sometimes the objection voiced is not the real one. Perhaps the prospect does not wish to share some information with the seller. Answering this type of surface objection without probing for the underlying reason results in additional surface objections and consequent postponing of a buying decision.

Selling Something the Prospect Doesn't Want

For example, you may assume that a business owner is primarily interested in saving money or reducing costs and base your presentation on showing evidence that your services provide those benefits. However, the prospect may be more concerned with looking good and with maintaining status and prestige and not at all cost conscious.

Selling is tough enough without creating your own stumbling blocks. Play the role of detective; learn to watch what is going on and be sure that you and the prospect are looking for the solution to the same problem.

54 Two Types Of Objections

When the prospect objects, you must understand what *type* of objection is being offered before you can handle it effectively. All objections may be separated into two general types. *Valid* or *real objections* are logical questions that may or may not be answerable. The prospect presents a real reason for not wanting to buy. *Invalid* or *false objections* are given to conceal the real reason for not wanting to buy. They are usually expressed as stalls or hidden objections.

Real Objections

One type of valid objection is what might be called a *stopper* or *condition without a solution.* For instance, if you can promise delivery no sooner than three months from now and the prospect absolutely must have the work in one month, you cannot—or at least, you should not—make that sale.

A second type of valid objection is a *searcher*, a request for additional information. It sounds like an objection, but is actually a request for more information.

- "Your offices are sure spread thin," probably means, "What evidence can you offer that you can service our global business?"
- "I am satisfied with my present lawyer" is more of an attitude than an objection. What the prospect means is, "I really haven't given much thought to changing."

To answer this type of objection effectively, you must have all the necessary product knowledge and be convinced that the prospect really can benefit from your service.

False Objections

A *false objection* may at first appear to be a valid, genuine one. When the prospect offers a *stall* or *put-off* objection, however, look for the true meaning. Frequently, the prospect is simply avoiding a decision. A stall is a classic sales killer unless you can create a sense of urgency to buy now. The objection is actually the prospect's way of saying "I really don't want to think about your proposition right now because I would then be forced to make a decision." Here are some examples of how stalls are phrased:

- "I have to leave in 15 minutes; I have an important meeting."
- "Just leave your literature with my secretary. I will look it over in the next day or so and then call you."

If you believe you have a qualified prospect whose needs will be satisfied by your service, then do not allow a *put-off* to put you off. Here are some suggestions for responding to stalls:

- "If you are too busy now, may I see you for 30 minutes this afternoon at 3:00, or would tomorrow morning at 9:00 be better?"
- "I certainly understand wanting to involve your partner in a decision like this. Can we ask him to join us now, or may I drop by his office this afternoon?"

Conclusion

The sale doesn't really start until you have objections. Learn to deal with these two types and you will be successful.

55 Techniques for Answering Objections

Here are three ways to strongly answer objections.

1. **Feel, Felt, Found**

   This practical technique overcomes a stall or a very personal objection. It can counter prospect hostility, pacify an unhappy client, or inform someone who does not yet clearly understand the value of the product or service. Answer the objection with this language:

   I can understand how you feel. . . . I have had other clients who felt the same way until they found out that . . .

   This approach serves several purposes. It shows the prospect that the seller understands the objection, and it reassures the prospect that having this kind of objection is normal. Then the stage is set to introduce information that can change the prospect's way of thinking. This technique says that other people who are now clients had similar misgivings but changed their minds after they considered new information.

2. **The Compensation or Counterbalance Method**

   In some instances, an objection is valid and unanswerable. The only logical approach is to admit that you cannot respond to the objection and exit as gracefully as possible. This individual is not a qualified prospect (for example, no need, no money). Do not waste your prospect's and your time trying to prove otherwise.

At times, however, a prospect may buy in spite of certain valid objections. Admit that your service does have the disadvantage that the prospect has noticed and then immediately point out how the objection is overshadowed by other specific benefits of the service. Your job is to convince the prospect that the compensating benefits provide enough value that the disadvantage should not prevent the prospect from buying. By admitting the objection, you impress the prospect with your sincerity and sense of fair dealing. This method works because the prospect is approached positively with an acknowledgment of expressed concerns, and then given a series of logical, compensating benefits to counterbalance the stated objection

3. Ask "Why?" or Ask a Specific Question
Asking questions is helpful not only for separating excuses from real objections but also for handling objections. You can use questions to narrow a major, generalized objection to specific points that are easier to handle. If the prospect says, "I don't like to do business with you," ask, "What is it that you don't like about our firm?" The answer may show a past misunderstanding that can be cleared up. If the prospect complains, "I don't like the look of your reports," ask, "What do you object to in their appearance?" The objection may be based on a relatively minor aspect that can be changed or is not true.

Conclusion

Being prepared to answer objections will make you more comfortable developing this important skill.

56 Handling the Price Objection

Do you often give discounts? If so, you may be losing more than just money. Successful selling creates a win-win situation: high profits for you and top value for your clients and prospects. If you don't defend your pricing, your clients and prospects may develop doubts about your value.

Pricing is an emotional as well as logical issue. Understanding your prospects' pricing emotions can help you to anticipate and handle price objections before they arise. There are three key price emotions:

- Price resistance
- Price anxiety
- Payment resistance

Be Prepared

Anticipating price resistance will enable you to be prepared with a strategy for handling the situation. Understanding how sticker shock and buyer's remorse occur just before and after a purchase decision will help you deal effectively with buyer anxiety. And payment resistance can be handled long before the check is cut.

Some buyers habitually ask for a discount from every provider of goods or services. Here are three strategies to maximize your pricing and your clients' perceptions of value:

1. **Don't telegraph your willingness to discount.** Business owners are savvy when it comes to purchasing goods and serv-

ices. If you let them know you have a policy of discounting, you are inviting a lengthy series of negotiations over price. As you are beginning your presentation, say something like, "We may not be the lowest priced firm in town, but that's not what you're looking for, is it?"

2. **Start your pricing at the highest expected amount.** Don't say, "We estimate our fees will be between $10,000 and $15,000." Say, "To do this right and achieve maximum value, I believe you may need to invest up to $15,000 with us." When you give a range, the prospect hears the low end while you are thinking the higher end. When you start at the high end, you leave room for concession.

3. **Discuss price only after you have created value in the client's mind.** Talk about your responsiveness, your network of business contacts, your satisfied clients and your firm's reputation before covering price. Show your prospect testimonial letters from happy clients. Create a perception of value, then cover price.

Conclusion

There are pricing pressures in every business. By being prepared to sell value, you can help keep your price—and your receivables—where they belong.

CHAPTER
TWELVE

Persuading Decision Influencers

57 Win Big with the "Strip Away"

One of the most exciting plays in football is the "strip away." A quarterback throws a perfect pass into the arms of his wide receiver, just to have the ball taken away—stripped away—by the free safety. The team that wins is usually the one that takes the ball away.

Stripping clients away from competitors is a game that only the best and most aggressive sellers can play. The strip away is not for the faint of heart. But, so long as you play within the rules, there are no ethical constraints.

Other Firms' Clients Aren't that Loyal

A Novak Marketing study showed that only 25% of CPA firm clients are intensely loyal to their firm. The other 75% were ambivalent or actively looking for another service provider. I think the same loyalty factor is also true of law firms.

If you are interested in playing the "strip away" once in a while, here are some tips:

1. **Don't accept the "I'm happy with ABC Firm" answer.** The status quo is never as permanent as it might seem. If you are a better fit, keep asking questions and discussing your firm's capabilities.

2. **Assume the prospect will switch if you can help him find a good reason.** Without this mindset, other tactics are not helpful.

3. **Find a small low-cost, low-risk service that is not being provided by the present firm.** For example, you might review

a person's will or her tax return with a fresh set of eyes or for a second opinion.

4. **Be alert for communicating new benefits.** If your firm develops a special expertise, or makes any change for the better, communicate "in person." Every time you promote a person to partner, find time to visit all your best prospects and introduce her. Find reasons to stay in touch.

5. **Look for changes.** If the controller leaves, if your competitor retires, you may have an opening to build a relationship on an equal footing with your competitor. Can any of your services help a client with changes they are experiencing?

6. **Keep track of company policy.** Some clients have a policy of formal rotation or of reviewing all supplier arrangements periodically. Know when that opportunity is to come up; ask for a chance then.

Summary

As with any relationship, the trick is to anticipate needs. Make sure that every prospect knows what you can do for them. Even, if they are truly being well served, when a problem arises, the prospect should know you could help solve it.

Lastly, keep trying. If a prospect is a good one, you should find ways to stay in touch. Invite the prospect to your office. Ask a friend to put in a good word for you. See if you have relationships with their other professionals. Place them on your newsletter list. Use your marketing system to keep your message in front of this prospect. Author Harvey Mackay said that few firms use the strategy of being the number two choice of clients that their competitors have locked up. If you are next in line, good clients will regularly fall into your lap.

58 Control the Sale with Better Questions

With decision makers and influencers, you will be better off letting them do most of the talking. You want to let them think they are in control, while you (like the puppeteer) hold the strings. The average person can think at about 600 words per minute (WPM) while he can only speak at about 125 WPM. So while you sit and talk to your prospect at 125 WPM, and she thinks at 600 WPM, how much of their attention do you think you are holding? About one fourth of it.

Don't take this personally! Have you taken any lecture-based CLE or CPE lately? Then you know the feeling. To be more successful at selling, try to involve your prospect throughout all phases of your sales call, even when you are making a so-called "presentation."

Questions Involve Prospects

Here are some questions you could ask a prospect during a sales call:

- "How do you define quality in a professional firm relationship?" While the vast majority of prospects will say things like, "I want a lawyer who understands my business," or, "I want an accountant who will help me get what I want," some will define quality in other ways.
- "What do you like most about the firm you are currently using?"

Finding Unmet Needs

If the prospect answers this question by giving her current firm extravagant praise, it may be she is only using you to shop for price. However, if she tells you about things she doesn't like, you can begin to pursue these topics until you discover unmet needs.

- "How do you think I might be able to help you?" The prospect is about to tell what benefits he expects from a relationship with you. Your sales presentation should then be built around proving you can deliver the prospect's expectations.
- "What are your goals and priorities over the next three years?" Can you help the prospect achieve any of his top goals? If so, you should focus your sales presentation on proving how you will be able to do it.
- "Who, besides you, would influence a decision to hire my firm? Would your bank have any input? Your board? Your family?"

To succeed, you must be known to the key decision maker and to as many decision influencers as possible.

Summary

Work to change your sales presentation by using questions that involve the prospect. Develop your own questions that fit your prospects and situation. For example, you can keep your prospect involved in your sales presentation by showing her a list of your references and asking her if she knows anyone on it.

59 Position Power Sells

The position power of your firm's managing partner (or CEO) is one of the most underutilized resources of a professional firm sales team. Bringing your CEO into a major sales call can create a winning edge in establishing a sincere, high-level relationship. Clients and prospects immediately feel more comfortable and important when the CEO of his or her professional firm visits.

One of Lou Gerstner's secrets to turning IBM around was the use of his personal and position power with large customers. Gerstner was reported to spend about 40% of his time meeting with IBM customers. He didn't handle any customers directly and he didn't get paid based on his "book of business." As CEO, he knew that his role impacted the entire company.

CEOs Can Help Sell

As a partner, you can benefit from having your CEO along with you. You will benefit by having another set of eyes and ears with you. Demonstrating that your prospect will have access to your senior executive can be very motivating for the prospect.

You can benefit from the coaching your CEO gives you, and she may benefit from the coaching you give her. If you take your CEO, it is good to write an agenda for each call. If the call begins to vary, or your CEO takes over, you can fall back to that neutral plan and get back on track.

CEOs Should Support Others Regularly

CEOs of professional firms who also carry a large book of business cannot devote time to helping the firm's partners with their largest clients and prospects. They cannot use their position power to help their firms grow.

If you are the CEO of your firm, I recommend you set aside a day per month to make client and prospect visits with each of your partners. Tell the partners ahead of time that you are available and let each of them plan out their own day to get maximum use of your time.

A CEO's presence at a proposal can create differentiation to help close an important sale. The presence of your CEO can often keep your clients from talking about price discounting. When you show how much you value the relationship by bringing your CEO, the client begins to value you more.

Summary

If your firm wants to improve its marketing, the effort has to start from the top. The managing partner should be a cheerleader, a source of rewards, and an inspiration.

60 Closing the Sale

Y ou may have invested months or years developing a relationship built on trust with a prospect. You do not want to
destroy the trust you have built by having your prospect feel like
you are strong-arming her. On the other hand, many prospects
will appreciate a nudge from you to begin working together. Executive decision influencers, in particular, are responsive to
closing statements or requests.

When you fail to ask the prospect for his business, he may
get the idea you are not interested. But, many novice sellers use
closing statements poorly. They use the statements too soon and
come across as pushy. Or they use the statements too late and
come across as disinterested.

Here are three closing techniques that may work for you
under the right circumstances:

1. **Direct close.**
   The direct close is the easiest to use. It requires little prepa-
   ration. A firm commitment to use the direct close appro-
   priately on sales calls after you completely understand the
   prospect's needs and wants will help you be more success-
   ful. Here are a few phrases you might use:
   - "There is only one question left. When would you like us
     to begin working for you?"
   - "Do I have your approval to go ahead with this sched-
     ule?"
   - "Does this agreement suit your expectations?"
   - "Do I understand you correctly that we have your busi-
     ness?"

2. **Sharp angle close.**

A huge mistake I see professionals make occurs when a prospect asks you a question about your ability to provide something. This request usually excites the novice seller into thinking you have a sale. The prospect says, "Could you represent us in tax court?" If you jump right back and say, "We sure can. My partner Bill has successfully represented many clients in tax court," you are missing a good opportunity to close.

A more appropriate response from you might be something like this: "If you knew we could do a good job in tax court for you, would that be a key decision factor in hiring us?"

3. **Change places close.**

This close asks your prospect what he would advise you to do to get the business. It goes something like this: "George, your company is a perfect fit for our firm. We help several clients just like you with their businesses. I really want to work with you. If you were in my shoes, what would you do to get you to say yes to our proposal?"

Conclusion

Don't be afraid to ask for the business. But when you do ask, pick the right time and method, and don't be pushy.

61 Try the "Puppy Dog Close"

Have you ever taken a puppy home "just for the night" to see how the kids like it? You now own it, don't you? After your family has spent a few hours with the puppy, you are hooked. The same is true with various products and services.

The "puppy dog close" works on the principle that once a person has experienced something for a short time, he or she hates to give it up. What about your services?

What Can You "Send Home"?

Can you think of a puppy dog close that would work? With a little creativity, any professional firm can create more sales using the puppy dog close. Three possibilities might be:

- A profit-improvement assessment
- A tax-savings review
- A trial use of one of your associates for a week

Here are the steps you can use to make the puppy dog close work for you:

1. **Sell the trial, not the service.** It is much easier to sell someone a tax-savings review than it is to sell a will update. Tell your prospect, "If you don't receive five times the dollars of profit ideas than your fee, the project will cost you nothing." Or you could price the service ridiculously low, say $1,000 for a three-day project. Don't give the service away unless there is no alternative.

2. **Gain the prospect's confidence.** Make it clear that this service does not create any obligation. During the trial period, your goal should be to get the prospect to like you and trust you. Just like the puppy dog, blink your big brown eyes at the kids, be fun to be around, and don't pee on the carpet!

3. **Bear hug the prospect.** During the "trial" period, you can turn on your winning ways to really get to know the prospect and the business. Your goal is to get the prospect to enjoy working with you. Work very hard to exceed the prospect's expectations. Develop profit ideas of ten times your fee, rather than five times. Find something you can implement quickly while you're there, especially some little job they've been putting off.

Use Your Findings to Close the Sale

If you have turned up any improved ways of doing business for your prospect, your prospect will be very open to hiring you. Help your prospect find reasons for engaging you by appealing to their buying motives and use the trial results as proof of the benefits of doing business with you.

Conclusion

Develop several ways to close the sale. The puppy dog close is one way to demonstrate what you can do for prospects.

62 Winning Proposals

A written document provides the financial and qualitative information necessary to make an informed engagement decision. While in most instances the written document is a small portion of the buying decision, it can be the deciding factor.

What Is a Winning Proposal?

A well-written proposal will first review the information the top decision influencers have shared with you about their issues and the value of solving their needs and wants. Capturing the specific value of changing service providers will present the financial logic to support a buying decision.

Top management is primarily concerned with profits. In many businesses, the technical aspects will be delegated to the user buying influence. A proposal should only contain the technical support necessary to support the business reasons.

How long should the written proposal be? The proposal should be long enough to cover the relevant aspects of solving the prospect's issues. Seventy percent of the length should be focused on the prospect and less than thirty percent on you and how great your firm is. You may want to ask the prospect how long the proposal might be. You may also simply put the proposal in an engagement letter format, so when the prospect signs you are in business.

How Do Buyers Choose You?

It is crucial for you to understand the buying conditions of each decision influencer and of the committee or group designated to make the decision. You will rarely have the luxury of interviewing each person on the committee, but you must do your best to have an audience with the person who has "big YES" authority. The committee should have established buying criteria such as reputation, number of similar clients in the industry, solid references, and good personal chemistry. In your proposal, you might list all the buying conditions and address your capability to deliver each one.

A key element in the written proposal process is for you to present your proposal in draft format to as many people in the decision process as possible. By presenting the written document and asking for feedback, you can hone the document and your understanding of the issues to a more precise solution.

Conclusion

Just as canned presentations and four-color brochures do not close the big sale, the boilerplate proposal does not work either. Boilerplate proposals are usually seller-oriented and will rarely impress your prospect.

Note: A lost proposal evaluation tool can be found in Appendix D.

THIRTEEN

Minimizing Risk

63 Support Your Proposal with Solid Evidence

When selling to key decision influencers, you will help the buyers to minimize risk when you can support your proposal with solid evidence for each of your claims.

Comparing Your Services

For example, when your prospect is mentally comparing his present service provider with your service, you may make a complete comparison of the two. List the advantages and disadvantages of working with each firm. In fact, you can get the prospect to do this for you by asking the right questions and leading her through the analysis.

When making a service comparison, you want to be overly fair to your competitor so you don't appear to be heaping negativity on the other firm in a biased way. But, you certainly want to get your prospect to talk about and amplify the reasons for changing firms. By getting the prospect to articulate the reasons for the change, you will be able to help him remember those reasons and perhaps remind his associates of those reasons.

The Costs of Delayed Decisions

Many people have an aversion to change and may need some help in overcoming this fear.

You could demonstrate the cost of delaying. Many businesses use professionals for many years after the business has outgrown the usefulness of the professional. But they are reluctant to change. By reviewing the lost profits or lost satisfaction or hassle factor, you can support your proposal with solid financial reasons to make a change to you. However, you want to focus on nonfinancial (qualitative) as well as financial reasons for clients working with you.

Types of Evidence

By relating a case history or showing a testimonial letter, you offer solid evidence of a good result. You should develop several good stories around successful client applications of your service. Better yet, ask your client to call the prospect and relay the story in his own words.

A guarantee often removes resistance by reassuring the prospect that the engagement will not result in a loss. Guarantees must be meaningful and must provide for recourse on the part of the customer if the service does not live up to the guarantee.

Conclusion

Buyers make decisions on emotion, then justify the decisions with logic. By providing solid evidence, your claims will stand the test of logic.

64 Minimize Prospect Risk with a Service Guarantee

At the moment of making a decision to hire you, many would-be clients balk. At the last minute, the decision process focuses on risk. "What are we risking to make this change," the CEO asks. Prospects fear change. The perceived risk of changing is often worse than staying with the known problems with their incumbent professional firm. I have witnessed many companies go out for bids, and then keep the same firm they are unhappy with.

How can you minimize fear and close the sale? By improving on the use of a tool you already have—the service guarantee.

Give a Guarantee Now!

Most advisors *essentially* give a guarantee now without reaping the benefits. Will you appease a complaining client? If your client is unhappy about his bill or your service, will you modify the bill or rework the service? If you stand behind your work, you are giving a service guarantee. But you are giving it after the fact, *not at a time when it will help you.*

You're missing a powerful marketing and practice aid when you use guarantees after the fact, rather than up front. Many professionals balk at the idea of giving a guarantee. Yet the word *guarantee* is one of the 12 most powerful in the English language, according to linguist Dorothy Leeds. When you guarantee satisfaction, you remove the risk inherent in the transaction. And you employ an attractive marketing tool at a point in the business transaction when it can get you the client.

Use Guarantees to Your Advantage

Bruce Horovitz, writing in *USA Today*, said, "There's one marketing tactic that's all but guaranteed to work every time: a guarantee." In practice I have found that a service guarantee goes beyond mere words. When you communicate that you have a service guarantee, you and your staff approach your work differently. Work is done with more care when everyone knows the work is guaranteed and that the client is the sole judge of its value.

A major Chicago law firm, Coffield, Ungaretti & Harris, advertised their guarantee in the *Wall Street Journal*. Partners attribute much of their firm's growth to the guarantee.

You're Not at Big Risk

Naturally, there are some caveats to implementing a service guarantee. No one can guarantee a result. If you have an unreasonable client or two, don't offer it to them. You may want to implement a service guarantee over a period of three years, and you should phrase a written guarantee carefully.

Conclusion

Advisory, accounting, and law firms are using guarantees more. The Rainmaker Academy has used one for over 10 years, guaranteeing satisfaction with everything we do. And we have made good on the guarantee twice during that time. I hope you will consider it in your future marketing plans.

65 Testimonials Minimize Perceived Risk

Receiving solid referrals from delighted clients is the best way to build your business. Your closing ratio will be very high with a referral, particularly if your referral source is a trusted friend of the prospect. The next strongest marketing tool is to utilize testimonials from great clients.

A third-party endorsement is one of the most persuasive marketing techniques around. Use testimonials in your advertising, in direct mail, in proposals, and in handout marketing materials. Clients love to do it for you and prospects are impressed.

How to Collect Testimonials

There are a variety of good ways to obtain good testimonials. You could simply ask your best and happiest clients to write testimonials for you. A better way is to send clients examples of what others have said or offer to write a testimonial for them. While written testimonials are the norm, there are more creative ways to collect and deliver them.

One firm hired a radio personality to perform live interviews of clients. The managing partner called about 10 clients and made appointments for the radio announcer. The announcer had a series of questions he asked each client. When he visited the clients, he took his time interviewing them. After each question, he asked the client, "Were you comfortable with your answer? Do you want to rerecord it?" Some clients recorded several answers to the same question so the firm would have a good selection. These testimonials provided excellent spontaneous material from which to build a commercial.

Using Testimonials

The managing partner identified the best comments from the interviews. They edited the tapes until they achieved a very tight 60 seconds of clients saying positive things about the firm, its partners, and services. During meetings with decision makers they play the 60-second version of about 20 very positive comments. Such a creative way of delivering testimonials is powerful and memorable. Many decision makers ask for a copy of the tape to play for others in the business.

Another effective way to use testimonials is to ask your client to call the prospect before your meeting. Ask him to talk directly to the prospect or leave a detailed voice mail. The prospect will be much more receptive.

A third way you could use a strong client endorsement is to request your delighted client to be available during the time of your prospect interview. Then at an appropriate time during the interview, say, "Bill Jones, one of our clients, has agreed to stand by to talk to you. He is waiting for our call right now. Would you mind if we called Bill and let him tell you first hand his experiences in working with us?" When the prospect agrees to this approach, you may volunteer to leave the room after the phone call has been connected.

Conclusion

Finding creative ways to use testimonials is a powerful selling tool and a way to minimize the perceived risk of working with you.

66 Lost Proposal Evaluations

After you have invested time in the proposal process and have lost, it is crucial to learn why. This gives you something in return for your efforts. If you can meet with the key decision makers to ask questions, you most likely will be able to gather a strong sense of what really occurred. If you cannot meet, set up time to conference call the key decision makers (all of them, if possible).

In some cases, it may be better to ask a savvy marketing director, another partner or an outside consultant to make the contact. Some clients will be less reluctant to tell a third party potentially sensitive information about you or the process.

Look for Consistent Patterns

You need to look at your track record over a number of proposal processes to really obtain a clear picture of how you are doing. Also, you must use your best judgment when evaluating comments. For example, on the same proposal, a CEO said it was too short and didn't fully address his issues and the CFO said it was too detailed. The real information we learned from a brief CEO interview was not about the length, but that the key issues of the CEO had not been addressed.

How to Analyze a Lost Proposal

Introduce yourself as follows: "Mr./Ms. Client, I'm _____ of _____. As you may recall, we recently proposed to _____ for your company. We were disappointed that we weren't chosen, because we invested a great deal of time in the proposal. However, we are happy that you feel you have a good solution for your situation. After we have proposed, we like to learn from the process in order that we may get better the next time. Would you take about 5 or 10 minutes with me to candidly answer some questions about the proposal we submitted. Your answers would be most helpful and I would be most grateful for you responding. May I ask a few questions?"

Conclusion

If you have lost a "beauty contest" for a new client, the biggest factor is usually that the prospect perceived lower risk in selecting your competitor. It is important that you evaluate the perceptions of the prospects and the risk perceptions they used to make the final selection.

Note: Appendix D contains an outline of a good lost proposal evaluation tool.

FOURTEEN

Great Service Builds Loyalty

67 Build Client Loyalty with Five-Star Service

Clients are more loyal to professionals who are proactive about providing service than ones who just react. Our five-star client service training is patterned after the service you receive at a five-star resort. The five-star client service system helps your firm reduce staff turnover, improve internal communication, raise the level of trust inside your firm, and ultimately achieve more loyalty from your clients.

In order to deliver five-star service, professionals focus on steps like the ones listed below.

Taking the Order

Waiters who take your order in fine restaurants have a big responsibility. Incorrect orders result in enormous cost increases from the rework of the food and customer dissatisfaction.

In a professional firm, when the order is not taken correctly, review notes and reworks abound. If you track your cost overruns and delivery delays, most of them would relate to not taking the order exactly. Many times a partner takes the order from the client and then plays "pass-it-on" to an associate. At each level of "pass-it-on" the message becomes garbled. The person lower on the totem pole does not want to press the issue of slight misunderstanding. He or she wants to move forward with the work and will do so without a clear picture of the order.

In order to take the order exactly correct, the partner must commit to a few more minutes with the client. It is necessary to listen carefully, take notes, and repeat the order back to the client. The associate must do the same, even though the partner may seem anxious and you may feel rushed.

Connecting

How would you feel if, after you have placed your order in a fine restaurant, the waiter did not check back with you? Many professionals commit this error for various reasons: tight work schedules, a fear that the initial order wasn't taken right, communication reluctance on the part of the service provider, a lack of care, or simply a lack of awareness of the importance of connecting with the client.

Connecting allows us to strengthen the relationship. We achieve this not only by simply keeping the client informed of progress and making contact, but by asking three simple questions:

1. *"What are we doing so far that you like?"*
2. *"Is there anything that we can improve on right now?"*
3. *"How do you feel about things so far?"*

These questions serve to uncover any hidden emotional concerns and problems before they occur. They also serve to strengthen the bond between you because the client feels attended to. Connecting also helps to overcome price anxiety, collect the fee, and plant the seed for further services.

Conclusion

Great service is dependable. Success in service excellence happens when you develop a system that delivers consistent, dependable responses every time.

68 Your Most Important Clients

Outstanding client service begins with the people you work with every day—your internal clients.

An internal client is an employee of your firm. For example, when a tax preparer compiles the return, he or she is the internal client of the partner who provides insight and guidance. And vice versa, as the partner reviews and signs the return, the partner is the internal client of anyone who may help in the processing of the return.

Delivering great service depends on keeping staff turnover low. As outlined in the book *The Customer Comes Second* (by Rosenbluth), reducing staff turnover and increasing staff satisfaction is the key to staff making clients happy.

Do Unto Others

Unfortunately, in both law and accounting firms, too often we witness a "Dr. Jekyll and Mr. Hyde" approach: the partner bends over backward for the external client, but takes internal clients for granted.

How external clients ultimately get treated is a direct reflection of how internal clients treat each other. As a business, you cannot give better service to your external clients than you do to your internal ones.

We are experiencing one of the most dynamic labor markets in history. Most law and accounting firms say their biggest need is not marketing, but finding qualified associates to do the work who have five to ten years of experience so they can hit the ground running.

Just this week, I worked with a large firm with the following characteristics: 10 partners, 50% travel, 70 staff members, average work year for all employees 2,600 hours. Employee compensation is average for the market, yet the firm had only lost three employees in the preceding two years. When asked about this excellent record, the employees said, "The partners treat each other with great trust and respect and they treat us the same way. Because we feel valued, this is a great place to work."

Treat Internal Clients with Respect

How can you expect to provide great service if you treat each other with disrespect? We thank our clients, and we always should try to thank our employees for providing good internal client service. Both those thank yous are equally important.

Conclusion

During a number of our training sessions, the professionals develop excellent client service ideas. These ideas apply equally to our internal clients: to make our clients feel respected and recognized in a variety of meaningful ways, to be more responsive by returning client phone calls within four business hours, and to keep clients better informed as to the progress of our work. You need analogous internal service standards.

69 Partners: Leaders In Service To Internal Clients

In the last chapter, you were reminded that the way people inside the firm treat each other greatly impacts how the employees of the organization treat clients. Both internal and external service initiatives must be coordinated.

Implementation of client service opportunities must begin with the partners. Norman Vincent Peale once remarked, "Nothing is more confusing than people who give good advice but set bad examples." It's important for partners to lead with verbal guidance, but it isn't enough. They also must lead with their actions.

Ron Zemke, in his book *Service America,* says "There must be a client-oriented culture in the organization, and it is the leader of the enterprise who must build and maintain this culture." The way employees are treated by partners greatly impacts how the employees of the organization treat clients.

Internal Service

As covered in the last strategy, external service starts with internal service and respectful treatment. Sometimes reinforcing the right norms takes forceful intervention.

A partner with a large international firm told me that when he was a manager, he called a partner in Chicago. The partner did not return the phone call. The manager called again the next day. Still, no return call was forthcoming. The manager reported to his own partner in Atlanta that the client matter was being delayed awaiting a response from the Chicago partner.

The Atlanta partner called the unresponsive Chicago partner, got him out of a meeting, and reminded him of the policy of respect for each other. And that respect included responding to any employee anywhere in the firm.

Role Modeling External Service

In law and accounting firms all across America where service is excellent, the partners do a lot more than tell employees what they want. They act as role models and show genuine concern for clients by taking time to listen and help them. And they back up their commitment to client service by looking for, measuring, recognizing, and rewarding performance that results in good service at all levels and in all jobs.

We don't want to support the old proverb that familiarity breeds contempt. Rather than breeding contempt, we really want to look for the good in others and use that good to provide great service to our clients. Recognition and praise are two of the most powerful motivators of all, yet you'd think that paying someone a compliment costs $1,000.

Conclusion

If you see any other employee without a smile, give her one of yours, and maybe she will pass it on to one of your clients. If you see any opportunity for improvements in this area of your firm, perhaps your training programs should emphasize internal client service this year as the basis for great external service.

70 Consistent Service Builds Brand Loyalty

Service consistency is a goal most midsized professional firms strive toward. It provides control over your customer service. It is also a great reason to contact your clients.

The journey to firm-wide consistency is difficult because of the lack of communication with existing clients about the quality of the current service being delivered.

None of us wants to hear bad news, but talking with clients is crucial. The difference between a satisfied client and a highly satisfied client can be night and day. For instance, Xerox found that customers who rated them a 5 on a 5-point satisfaction scale were six times more likely to purchase further products than customers who rated them a 4! Accountants seem content to send out useless client surveys in the mail, but hesitate to go see the clients personally.

Standards of Service

The only way to establish service consistency is for the owners of a firm to set down the service laws:

- Promptness in dealing with client concerns
- Maintaining client comfort in difficult circumstances
- Ensuring regular communications during engagements
- No training of junior staff on client's nickel

Develop Consistency

For every significant engagement, the managing partner or marketing professional should visit the client and ask the two key questions: How did we do? How can we get better for you?

The service consistency equation becomes more difficult when a firm is focused on growing inexperienced staff members. Will each one of them be able to deliver fine service consistently, or must an owner always be present? McDonald's delivers a consistent product with minimum-wage employees because they have clear service standards and train the team members to deliver your food the same way, every time.

Conclusion

Before advertising your service excellence, make sure that you can deliver services consistently and that your whole team is on board.

71 Client Satisfaction Surveys Are Passé

The client satisfaction survey is one of the most misused marketing tools employed today. Most surveys fail to obtain reliable information. Even worse, many surveys obtain misleading information.

The single most important reason to perform a survey is to determine client intentions. What your clients say doesn't always equal intentions. A few years ago, in a focus group, Sony Corporation asked teenagers which color of boom box they would prefer? Black or yellow? The overwhelming response was yellow. At the end of the three-hour session, the teens were told they could pick up their choice of a free boom box as a gift for participating in the focus group. The overwhelming choice was black! The key to client intention is not what people say, it's what they do.

Ask Questions that Deal with Client Intentions

Following are a few ideas to improve your use of client surveys so the information you receive is more reliable and useful:

- *"Will you come back to us for your next need?"*
- *"Have you or will you refer us?"*
- *"Would you use us for other services?"*

Use questions like these to reveal client intentions.

Design a Competent Survey Methodology

Professionals who understand anything at all about statistical sampling realize that a 35% response rate from clients probably does not reflect the true responses of your client base. Were the responses from your best clients or your worst clients? Were the responses completed by decision makers or influencers of your clients?

Use a methodology that will give you reliable feedback on your most important clients. Personal or telephone interviews of your largest clients will receive a much higher percentage response rate than mail surveys. If you insist on using a mail survey, at least send a gift to reward your client for completing the questionnaire for you.

Ask Yourself, "Should We Do a Survey?"

If you do business with a limited number of clients and send them a survey every year, you will create survey burnout. If your clients have a complaint about your service, your people, or your billing methods, many will not want to put it in writing. You may be better off to visit your clients individually and explore their perceptions in-depth. All clients' comments are not created equal. But in a typical mail survey, a $300 tax return client's responses receive the same weight as a client who pays you $100,000 per year.

Conclusion

Surveys offer little chance of discovering anything unexpected over and above the topics being queried. The problem with this is that your own thinking contaminates and limits the thinking of your clients.

Surveys can be useful tools to help firms grow and respond competitively to the marketplace. But to gain new information, you must be careful to design a process that will give you useful and reliable information.

72 When Your Client Hires a New Chief

When a new CEO, COO, CIO, or CFO joins your client, your relationship may be at high risk. Smart professionals never take a client for granted, but they are particularly sensitive when there is a change in top management. In many cases, the new chief will not know you and probably will have some level of loyalty to another firm. Your key is to make life easier for the new chief.

Be Proactive

If your first reaction is to lay low, or to wait for the new chief to call you, this is the wrong approach. You should be proactive in building communication links. Your first role is to educate the new chief by reviewing the services your firm has provided the client. Show how you have had an impact on past cost savings, legal structure, business success, or other significant events. It is good insurance for you to review the past while emphasizing the reasons why you should continue.

Most new chiefs will bring new ideas, new initiatives, and a new team to their new roles. Some chiefs' approaches may be radically different from their predecessors. So, you don't want to represent the "old way." If you have had significant management or internal control recommendations, bring them up early in the new chief's tenure.

Increase Communications

Professionals who have weathered management changes offer some good suggestions:

1. **Begin to mentally prepare your next proposal to your client.** If the new chief has a relationship with another professional, they are probably asking for an opportunity. You would do this if one of your best friends took over a new client.

2. **Don't assume that business will go on as usual.** You must give more attention to the client's personnel with whom you have worked. You may be asked to alter your services package to suit a new direction for your client. It will be better for you to be a part of this planning process, if you can engineer it.

3. **The quickest way to alienate a newcomer is to act superior or overconfident.** Treat the new chief with great respect. You must recognize the new chief's ability and stress your wish to serve in the new environment.

When Family Members Become the Chief

The time to build relationships with family members who may become the chief is months or years before they are promoted. Often, successful CPAs have built strong relationships with the elder chief and avoided the children. Meanwhile, the children are forming their own relationships. Perhaps, now is a good time to focus attention on the sons and daughters of your client's owners.

Conclusion

A change in leadership is a time of both danger and opportunity. If you are mentally prepared and build your relationships broadly within your client firms, you will be better positioned.

73 Do You Have Second-Class Clients?

On a plane from Orlando to New York, I sat beside a meeting planner for PricewaterhouseCoopers. She told me a story that bears repeating.

The meeting planner had asked the catering department at Disney World to prepare an event for the PwC partners. Disney's caterer priced the affair at $50,000. But the meeting planner's budget was $35,000. Disney dropped its price.

Later during the event, the PwC meeting planner noticed that every item in the original event was included in the program. She mentioned this, with great appreciation and astonishment, to the Disney caterer. His reply was, "Disney may reduce our price, but we never will reduce our service."

Clients Who Pay Less

How do you handle clients who cannot pay your first-class price? Many times, I have observed these clients receiving second-class pricing and third-class service. Often, partners and others resent the discounts afforded some clients. Discounting and resentment often lead to a downward spiral of service and even greater discounts or to unhappy and lost clients.

You would be better off avoiding low-class service to any client. The undertone of resentment by the partner and staff will be transmitted to your client personnel in many ways. Slower phone call returns, slower reporting, lack of a management letter, and yearly staff turnover occur when you resent your lower fees.

How to Serve Budget Clients

A better approach would be to provide the same excellent service to your budget paying clients as you do to your first-class ones. But, how can this be possible? "Everyone cannot be treated like my number one client," you may say.

The way to make this work is to create trade-offs with your discounted clients. For example, determine if the work can be performed during a period of your year when a premium is not charged. Determine if the work can be staffed and managed by a lower billing rate individual. Determine if the work can be a joint venture with another firm, so you can spread the discount.

Commit to first-class service for all your clients: meeting your promised deadlines, promptly returning phone calls, making unsolicited visits and phone calls, maintaining continuity of staff, and providing management recommendations to your discounted clients. If you cannot make money on a client, it may be better to not serve the client than to give them second-class service.

Conclusion

I have witnessed numerous discounted clients willingly increase the fee structure when high quality is received. After all, before they started, they didn't know what to expect, and thus were cautious about costs. Most clients leave firms because the value and level of service is not up to the pricing. Don't let yourself fall into the downward service spiral of some professionals.

Use the Disney motto, "We may reduce our price, but we will not reduce our level of service."

Building Profits

74 A Client Business Review

A key marketing technique used by some top firms is the client business review (CBR). The CBR is used only on the firm's "top 25" accounts, defined by the total size of the annual fees, referral potential, or other criteria.

The CBR takes a business consulting approach to understand and evaluate the systems of your clients. The CBR usually requires about 20 hours per client and is done about every two years. Clients whose businesses are rapidly growing or changing may warrant a more frequent CBR.

Building Client Loyalty

If there is a question of loyalty, during the CBR the client will give you an opportunity to cure the problem, long before they tell your competitor. One attorney said, "But what if I bring up an issue where the client had not been unhappy until I mentioned it." It's better that this issue surface with you than your client bring it up with your competitor! When you hold a CBR, you will thwart most competitive advances on your territory.

Your Return on Investment

There are many additional benefits associated with a CBR. It is a way to train staff to market to clients. Well-trained staff can perform the CBR on second-tier "top 25" clients with less partner and total time invested. A CBR will increase the satisfaction level of a client from "satisfied" to "delighted." And, delighted clients are the ones who provide the best referrals.

The payback on the CBR program is consistently 5:1, whereas that with the new client sales program is about 2:1. In almost every situation, you will come away with a project on which significant fees can be generated. The cross-selling opportunities are endless. Additionally, the CBR program is protecting the large percentage of your fees (over 50%) from your key clients. Your new client marketing program starts each year at zero.

Most of the CBRs are performed during your slow periods, so that the real out-of-pocket investment is usually only the cost of lunch. So on a $20,000 client, a 6% marketing investment (about $2,400 in time) is made and on a $150,000 client, a 1.6% investment is made (done every year).

Summary

Doing a client business review with your best clients will elevate your level of service so that you can make a contribution to your client's business and organizational decisions. When you make an impact in this manner, you will protect your client loyalty and improve your realization rate. When you can help your clients achieve their strategic and financial goals, you become an indispensable part of their team.

Note: Appendix E contains an example of a Client Business Review Checklist.

75 Market Pricing Based On Value

Pricing is one of the four Ps of marketing and is one that few professionals use. Accounting and law firm marketing has improved over the past 20 years in three of the Ps of marketing (place, product, and promotion). But pricing is still being done using cost-accounting techniques.

Limits of Hourly Billing

Most clients hate hourly billing and will be very willing to alter the way they work with you. Ron Baker's book *The Professional's Guide to Value Pricing* is one of the more intelligent and informative books on the subject. His is a foundational book, one that comes along at an important time: a time when people are looking for a new direction, when paradigms are shifting.

Some of your clients are quite willing to pay you more than your are receiving from them, but you are failing to maximize your profits. For example, there are people who choose to drive luxury cars, when more affordable transportation is available. These same types of clients would pay you more if you designed a pricing system to capture what they are willing to pay for your results.

Other Fee Approaches

Commissions and contingent fees will become the norm within the next 20 years. But, there are alternatives to commissions and contingent fees.

To obtain higher pricing, you must focus more on providing value that clients want. The profitability to you and your client of various pricing methods will help you focus your attention on achieving both.

Using a fixed-price agreement combined with a change order system is one method we can all use to improve our pricing. Spelling out what you will and won't do for your fixed price is the essence of a fixed-price agreement. Items not covered in the agreement are changes, just as your builder does with your home as it progresses.

Conclusion

If you bill by the hour, to make more money you have to work longer hours. If you bill by value delivered, you have the chance to make more income, and focus on client satisfaction. For instance, one firm specializes in "Starker" exchanges of real estate. (People avoid taxes by trading one investment property for another, without having to make the trade themselves.) Fees for changing a $1,000,000 taxable event into a tax-free transaction are based on the expertise involved, not on the hours.

76 Cycle Selling with Clients and Prospects

If you are like most attorneys, consultants, and accountants, many of your clients utilize only a few of your services. Too often, a client engages another professional to perform services that you could provide. Cross-selling is when you sell a new service to an existing client. Cycle selling does this in a more complete and systematic way that can become an automatic way of increasing your business.

In a Weber State University study of why clients switched CPAs, the number one reason given for switching was that the CPA was not proactive in delivering services. You can be proactive in delivering services if you will adopt the cycle selling method.

Let Clients Know What You Offer

You know that selling to existing clients is far easier and more profitable than developing a new client. To ensure that you are providing all the services possible, take advantage of cycle selling. For each client, maintain a listing of all your services, perhaps in the front of a permanent file. Then, over a period of two to five years, present each service to your client. Keep notes of your actual conversations with the client and what resulted from your exchange. This cycle selling concept is not a one-time only proposition; you should keep updating your list of services, and keep reviewing your capabilities with your clients year after year. Your bottom-line strategy is to make sure that all your clients are aware of all your service capabilities.

Never Assume Clients Don't Need Certain Services

And don't overlook the services that fall into the category of "He (or she) will never need this." Instead, say something like this: "Mr. Jones, you may never have a need for the service I want to tell you about, but I would be remiss if you weren't aware of all of our capabilities." You never know when this will create a referral to someone who does need the service. And, by discussing services that you know won't be needed, you remove sales pressure. This builds into the relationship the expectation that you will share what you do with the client. You can even use such discussions as a forum for soliciting advice about the service, or who would need it.

Your newsletter can also support cycle selling. Over time it can feature different clients benefiting from different services, but your personal presentations will have more impact.

Create a System

Present only two new services at a time. Most people are unable to absorb and retain much information at once. Depending on many factors, you could present two services every three or six months. Develop a system to make it a natural part of your relationship building with each client and you will build your business along with client satisfaction.

Offering Dessert

77 Offering Dessert, Going For Gold

*by Graham G. Wilson**

Recently, I was sitting with a client in a "chain" restaurant. Our waitress was well mannered, knowledgeable, and polite. We enjoyed our salad, a fantastic steak, and a glass of wine. We were all quite satisfied. At the end of the meal, as our waitress cleared away the empty plates, she asked, "Any room for dessert?" While the option was there, we did not (and could not) take her up on her kind offer. We paid and left.

What was missing, both for us as customers and for her as a service provider?

Yes, dessert was the key element that was missing—not because it was not offered—but because the offer came too late in the dinner. Since we had not been thinking about dessert or mulling over in our minds the wonderful flavors of a soufflé, it was easy to say no.

The Art of Offering

For professionals, offering additional services to your client is similar to offering dessert. There is an art to success.

Successful restaurants, and professional service firms, offer dessert early in your dining experience. Some have desserts tantalizingly displayed on a cart that you must walk by as you go to your table. Capture my imagination and you will capture my willingness to engage you further. By sowing the "seeds of a

*Graham G. Wilson is a consultant with The Rainmaker Academy.

need" early in the relationship, I am more likely to expand the engagement beyond the initial service needed.

On the other hand, if dessert is not offered, we would all be disappointed. We would think something is missing from our experience. Your clients feel the same way. Have you ever had a client say, with an edge, "I didn't know you did that"? Imagine your disappointment when you later learn the client has done his estate planning with another professional, when he could have done it with you.

Dessert = Extra

But why is dessert so important? Because this is where higher levels of profit for you and the client exist but are rarely tapped. In any fine restaurant, the chef will tell you that higher profit is made from dessert than the entrée. It is cheaper to prepare and sells at a premium price. The analogy is equally important in any professional services firm. Often, in the first year of a new engagement, little (if any) profit is made; however, if dessert (additional value-added service) is offered early in the relationship, the client is already presold and a premium price may be asked.

Summary

Your clients are looking for "one-stop" shopping. Offering dessert is a way of maximizing profitability, enhancing relationships, and ensuring that your clients are left with a "good taste" in their mouths. *Bon appetit!*

78 Premium Services

Attorneys and CPAs are privy to more information about their clients' business affairs than any other professionals. You have the powerful potential to add real value to your client relationships.

One key area in which you can add value is in helping your clients visualize their business futures. You are uniquely qualified to help clients with business strategic planning, personal financial planning, tax planning, technology planning, and many other types of forward-thinking strategies.

Sell Top Value

Most clients will tell you that business planning ranks near the top of the "value ladder." Commodity services are on the bottom rung and services with high impact rates are at the top of the ladder. In between the bottom and top rungs are various stages of value in services. Price resistance is highest at the bottom of the ladder, and competition is stiffest. Near the top of the ladder, both competition and price resistance fade away.

Some experts will tell you, "Accounting and law are moving away from compliance services." I say, "Not true." It is true that most compliance services are commodity-like in nature and therefore reside near the bottom of the value ladder. However, if you add only 20% in high-value services into your mix, you can collect premium fees on the commodities. You will also experience a noticeable decrease in fee complaints.

What Premium Services Can You Offer?

For example, strategic planning is a value-added service you can help provide clients. Encourage your larger clients to hold an annual planning advance (what has traditionally been called a "retreat"). Perhaps you could facilitate the advance. Certainly you should attend and contribute to the dialog. You can help with projections or forecasting. Many business people are excellent at visualizing their futures, but many are not good at the in-depth thinking and calculating necessary to develop a strong plan. You can help. When you help clients plan for their business futures and keep track of their pasts, you will become a true full-service professional.

Another service offering is personal financial planning and tax planning. They are value-added services that other businesses have taken away from the accountants and attorneys. Many of us have been so busy protecting our low-end commodity services that banks, consultants, insurance companies, and others have become well known for these services.

Summary

CPAs and attorneys have unique qualifications. Talk with your clients about helping plan their business futures. Many of them will welcome your suggestions and you will increase your position of trust and profits.

79 Use the Summary Close with Clients

The summary close is especially useful when you are offering a new service to one of your existing clients. (Sales to existing clients are the most profitable.) When you approach the end of your presentation, your client is faced with the task of organizing all the pieces of information into one clear and comprehensive picture. The summary close is excellent to use in this situation, because it is a logical organization of the features and benefits. With the summary close, you are partnering in the decision-making process with your client.

Help Them Decide

Although your client may be very impressed with your vast knowledge, he or she may experience some difficulty organizing what you have said. In essence, the summary close is designed to refocus your prospect's thinking on a composite picture of those parts of your presentation that clearly fit his or her needs.

Amateur sellers tend to think of the summary close as a quick review of what they like best about the services. They fail to match the summary close to the buyer's specific situation, and then wonder why the client didn't buy.

How to Do It

There are four separate steps to a successful summary close:

1. **Introduce the close with a smooth tie-back statement.** Say something like, "Tom, I realize we have covered many as-

pects of the like-kind exchange technique. Why don't we take a few moments and summarize the salient points?" With a good transition statement, you have prepared the client for the review.

2. **Briefly reconfirm your prospect's specific needs.** You might say it like this: "Tom, you have a very low basis in the real estate you want to sell. When you sell it outright, you will pay a substantial tax. What we are trying to avoid is paying all that tax right now. This is what you'd like to do, right?"

3. **Summarize how the benefits of your features meet the client's explicit needs.** Some professionals use a T-account (summarizing the pluses and minuses for a decision on one sheet) so you and the client will agree on the pros and cons of making the decision.

4. **Ask for the business using a direct request.** When you have completed the summary, now it is time to close. You might ask something like this, "Our tax expert, Jeremy, is available to work on this next week. Shall I reserve his time for this project?"

I use the summary close with clients. I tie back to a stated need, state a feature of how to solve that need, a benefit of doing so, and a reconfirming question to keep the client/prospect engaged. It is very helpful in staying focused and engaged with the client/prospect.

—Christina Ricke, Kennedy & Coe, Wichita, Kansas

Conclusion

A summary close helps clients understand what you have to offer. And it helps build your profits by making the sale.

SEVENTEEN

Soliciting Referrals

80 Client Referrals

You know that referrals are the best way to get new clients. To get the best referrals, you need more than naturally occurring word of mouth. You need to have a program to actively encourage referrals in multiple ways.

You'd think that clients would give you referrals because they like you or your service. However, it doesn't always happen this way. To have a top practice you must do more than produce good work and wait for referrals to follow.

Some clients are just more likely to give referrals than are others. When you identify someone who is liberal with their referrals, cultivate them. They will be worth several people who like you just as much but aren't in the habit of giving referrals.

Ask for Referrals

You need to set up a regular system of asking for referrals. In addition to calling current clients and asking them for referrals, you can call past clients and ask them for the names of people who might need your service. Often they also turn out to be interested in trying you again.

A good time to ask for referrals is when people compliment you. A woman said that her clients sometimes thank her effusively for helping them with their money situations. She tells them "The best way to thank me is to send your friends who might need the same help."

Reward Referrals

While you can't "pay" people for referrals, you can reward them in some ways. One accountant holds an annual dinner for his referral relationships. After dinner, he takes a few moments to thank everyone for sending referrals. A lawyer I work with always sends a letter of appreciation. You certainly should thank them and try to send them referrals in turn, so long as the quality of work and reputation is of high caliber. Or you may be able to do business with them yourself. You can also arrange meetings between clients who might do business with each other.

Conclusion

You may think of asking for referrals as an admission of weakness—that you want more business. But if you don't ask for referrals, why should people assume that you want them? If you're established in business, you need to be clear that you want more business. Asking can also show your strength. People understand that you may want to grow your business, or obtain more clients of a certain type.

81 The ABCs of RSD—Referral Source Development

by Patrick Patterson*

Do you have anyone in your circle of relationships, business or professional, who would say great things about you? Perhaps even say them to a potential prospect? If you do, congratulations—consider them a treasured source, real gems with which to work. If not, why not?

How to Spell Referral

The earliest recorded use of the word *referral* in the professions was in 1927. It's been around awhile. Maybe it's time to rediscover it again.

Here is a simple summary of referral source development basics:

- **Relationships.** Relationships are the key concept in RSD. The quality and quantity of referrals you get depends on the quality and quantity of the referrals you give! Referral marketing works because within these relationships, the goal is mutual benefit.

- **Engagement.** Teaching your referral source how to engage a prospect in a first contact, on your behalf, has the most significant impact on your later success in converting them to clients. Always remember: someone else can "sell" you better than you can sell yourself.

---

*Patrick Patterson is a consultant with The Rainmaker Academy.

- **Follow-up.** After the source talks with the prospect, more follow-up may be appropriate. First, from the source, with further verbal or written information (materials you have thoughtfully provided to your source). Then you meet with the prospect soon thereafter, ideally with an introduction from your source.

- **Evaluation.** Analyze the activities and results of your RSD all along the way and you'll be able to tell what to stop, start, and continue doing!

- **Recognition.** It's important to recognize your sources—both at the time the referral is made and certainly after a referral has become a client. Keep your referral sources informed.

- **Rewards.** Establish a *consistent* reward program that demonstrates your appreciation. Rewards would include thank you letters or phone calls, or having them visit your firm and meet with your partners. You may ask them to attend CPE or CLE courses your firm sponsors. You should not, however, pay for referrals. If you sometimes reward certain actions and sometimes not, your sources may consider you ungrateful or unreliable and, certainly, inconsistent.

- **Advising.** Provide your sources with valuable advice. Make them confident that you are an important source for them and referees.

- **Leadership.** RSD requires self-leadership. Stay with your RSD efforts for the long run.

- **Service.** Continuously seek and find ways to serve your best sources.

Conclusion

If you have not yet realized the *vital* role of RSD in the long-term success of your practice, use this formula to set up a system that works for you.

For more details on all these points, I would like to *refer* you to Meisner and Davis's *Business by Referral.*

82 Build Referrals Naturally

The most profitable marketing activity in which you can engage is building referrals. And the best way to develop referrals is getting to know all the other professionals—the bankers, bonding agents, insurance brokers, accountants, lawyers, and so on—whom your present clients utilize.

These other professionals have a natural inclination to help their clients' businesses. And, that includes meeting with you to generate new ideas for the benefit of your mutual client. During the brainstorming, business relationships get built that lead to referrals for you.

Most referrals come from people who are impressed with your work and who trust you to handle their friend well. There are three great ways to stimulate your referral sources to send you business.

Ask for a Referral

Many professionals I've met say they don't want to offend their good clients by "hitting on" them for new work. The truth is the person is really too timid to ask for the referral. Every person enjoys the feeling of doing something for someone they like. So, don't deprive your good clients of this pleasure.

Some of your clients may think you don't have room for another client. Let them know your doors are open for business by asking for a referral. Several successful firms will write a letter periodically asking for referrals to about a third of their clients annually. (See Appendix F for an example of a good letter.)

Enhance their Revenue

When you get to know your clients' other service providers well, you can find ways to enhance their revenue. Send them a referral, include them as a team member on decisions affecting your mutual client, or do business with them.

When you enhance their revenue, you create a due bill of which you will be the beneficiary.

Stay in Contact

Asking for a referral may be difficult for a timid professional. And opportunities to enhance others' revenue may be limited. But anyone can stay in touch.

In many interviews I've conducted with people who refer to professionals, they tell me they send most referrals to the professional they think of first. That means that the person who stays in touch regularly through a newsletter program, a letter campaign, a seminar, personal visits, phone calls, or for any business reason is going to capture a portion of the referral source's mind. When you capture a share of the mind, you will get a share of their referrals.

Note: Appendix G provides a checklist on ways to stay in touch with different types of referral sources.

83 Developing Referral Relationships

Some referral relationships will develop quickly once you've made contact with someone who refers to providers in your area regularly. Other relationships will take years to develop fully. After you've make contact with a potential referral source, you need a system to follow up and build the relationship.

One of the first things you want to find out is the extent to which your new contacts actually refer clients to others.

Prioritize Your Efforts

I use an ABC system for rating new referral sources. You can also apply this rating and follow-up system to people you've known for a while. They also vary in their potential as referral sources.

The next step depends on whether you've classified them as an "A," "B," or "C" potential referral source.

A "C" contact is one who says he or she rarely refers clients to other professionals, or one who has a well-established relationship with a competitor of yours. About half the people you meet will be "Cs," at least initially.

Follow up with these people by putting them on an email or newsletter list, invite them to your seminars, and practice other low-cost ways of staying in touch. Some will warm up over time, and some will end their relationships with your competitors.

A "B" contact is one who might be able to make one to five referrals to you each year. He may have a relationship with another firm, but you sense potential. Initially, as many as 40% of the people you meet will be "Bs."

Follow up with this group as with the "Cs," plus. Contact them twice a year, just to stay in touch, and—if your talks prove fruitful—schedule another face-to-face meeting.

Your Best Contacts

An "A" contact either needs services for his or her own practice or has the opportunity to refer clients to you more than five times a year. Of course, you probably won't meet too many of these—probably about 10% percent of all the contacts you make will begin as "A" contacts. But, for these few, you will want to undertake the highest level of follow-up.

Conclusion

Prioritizing your potential referral sources is the first step to more efficiently reaping referrals.

84. Making the Most of Your Prioritized Prospects

Once you've prioritized your referral contacts, the next step is to make an effort to build the relationships with low-priority contacts and to directly encourage referrals with your most likely prospects.

Refining Your Follow-up System

One accountant specifically budgeted the follow-up for each type of referral source. His "C" sources received his quarterly newsletter. The accountant sent his "B" sources the quarterly newsletter plus, once a year, a business book with a personal note explaining why the book is of interest. His "A" sources received the newsletter plus a book every quarter.

"Hot" Referral Possibilities

There is a momentum to relationships. When you meet someone who has "A" referral potential, follow up immediately. For instance, invite the "A" prospect to your office right away. To convince them that he or she will also benefit from such a meeting, you might say, "Our associates are always looking for excellent people to whom we can send our clients. Could you come by for an informal meeting?"

Prioritizing your potential referral sources is the first step to more efficiently reap referrals. What are the objectives of this second meeting? First, to communicate how your firm is different—and better—than your competitors. And second, perhaps to ask for a referral.

If during this meeting you discover that the person is in reality a "B," you might say something like this: "We share many clients with professionals just like you, and we hear they like our service. If you have an opportunity to refer one of your clients, I assure you they will receive the best personal service I can provide." Upon saying this, wait for a response. Many times, the response will be, "We send our clients to Smith & Jones." Respond by saying, "I'm glad you respect them so much. I hope one day to earn your trust and I'm willing to wait for you to be comfortable with me."

Time Builds Relationships

For "A" prospects, you can afford to take a more subtle approach. Take the time to get to know their practices better, introduce them to all of your associates, and establish mutual trust and rapport. Make the effort to keep in contact; research shows that they will become more comfortable with you over time.

After the first meeting, here are three possible next steps you can take.

- Invite your new business friend to meet with a client who may be a good match for them.
- Offer to host a "mixer" for all their associates.
- Invite them to an upcoming special event, such as a play, concert, or sports event.

There are other ways to expand the relationship, such as attending a group they already attend or exploring an interest you have in common. At this juncture, it is vital that you move to enhance the relationship. Do not let the relationship drop now.

Conclusion

Once you have established relationships with "A" sources, referrals and joint business should come naturally.

85 Panels Get Staff Involved in Referral Development

If you've been looking for ways to encourage staff members to ask for referrals, they might appreciate a few pointers from the clients and professionals they would be approaching. Information direct from the "horse's mouth" will always have more impact than what you might tell them.

When you've established a solid relationship with another professional firm in your town, you might want to ask them to serve on a panel discussion attended by your staff. Invite the professionals to tell your staff members how they like to be asked for referrals. You may even be able to obtain a panelist who is a staff member at another professional firm. They can provide an ideal role model for your staff. Encourage the panelists to provide specific stories and examples of people who receive their referrals.

Five Keys to Referrals

I recently worked with a panel of attorneys to help CPAs stimulate their referrals. Much of what they said would apply to any professionals.

1. **Work from your strengths.**
    People who are overly cautious will not earn respect. Help your referral source anticipate the future and prevent problems. As a staff member, your statements about your firm are given more credibility than the partners'. Provide a balanced picture while still plugging your firm's strengths.

2. **Talk results.**
   Vague statements about quality don't impress people. Give them clear examples of ways your firm has made a difference for clients.

3. **Shoot straight.**
   Be up front about any problems or limitations of your firm. It builds your credibility.

4. **Understand your referral sources' needs.**
   Talk to potential referral sources about how to improve their own profits and how to satisfy their goals.

5. **Share your professional expertise.**
   Advise your referral sources on how to use your firm's services to their benefit. Give away "free samples" when possible.

Asking for Referrals

Many professionals and staff, as a group, are timid and fear asking for business. There are ways to ask without being aggressive. When you are meeting professionals or their staff, you must express your personal style.

In general, to build rapport with a referral source, you need to understand their style and approach them in a way that will be comfortable for them.

Conclusion

Some of your best referrals will come from happy staff. When your staff give you referrals, they have more credibility than when you ask for the business directly. They are seen as relatively objective sources of information.

EIGHTEEN

Becoming an Insider

86 Becoming an Insider

Professionals who are involved in attest services cannot afford the appearance of also being an insider with their clients. It is mandatory that accountants who are involved in attest work never allow their independence to be compromised. You must abide by the code of ethics of your profession, as well as state and federal rules regarding independence.

The strongest and most profitable relationships with clients are those in which you are considered an insider. When your and your clients' interests are assumed to be the same, you are treated as one of the team rather than an outsider who has to prove himself. As I see it, there are three distinct levels of being an insider:

- **Level 1**—The advisor can be an insider, if top management of your clients always checks with you prior to making important decisions. Your clients trust you and rely on your perspective before deciding to act. Being accepted as an advisor may be an indication that your client would be receptive to level 2 insider status for you.

- **Level 2**—The counselor is an insider who generally sits in on all key management meetings and participates from start to finish in the decision-making process. From time to time, the counselor may take the lead in organizing planning meetings, conducting strategic advances, and negotiating contracts with your client's customers.

- **Level 3**—The Partner Leader is an insider who functions as a part-time chief: CEO, CFO, CIO, CAO, or CMO. Many accountants and attorneys function in such a role, sometimes without title. Operating as a partner leader, you have the ability to inject forward-thinking strategy into the top management of your clients.

Being a Deep Insider

Many companies cannot afford, nor do they need, a full-time CFO. For example, the price tag on a top-level CFO might be $500,000 per year. What the companies do need is $100,000 worth of a $500,000 talent. Instead, what many companies settle for is a $50,000 talent for which they pay $100,000. The same concept is true with the CAO. Attorneys who fill the role of part-time CAO provide the high-level talent at a fraction of the cost.

So how does one become a deep insider? Usually, the client makes the decision after some period of relationship building. You are more likely to be considered a candidate for this role if you are responsive, reliable, and creative for your client. You also must have your sights set on something more than just a sale. Author Jim Holden believes that sales effectiveness moves through several stages. The highest stage is insider status. With insider status you focus on helping the client in their markets as if you were an insider or partner with your client.

A great example is an insider status is the IBM and Federal Express alliance developed for service efficiency. Federal Express stocks IBM parts in the FedEx warehouses for faster fulfillment. FedEx is focused on the IBM customer's satisfaction with delivery of critical parts.

Conclusion

When you begin to focus on your client's strategic direction and customers, you will make yourself a candidate for deep insider status, perhaps as partner-leader.

87 Focus on Client Profits

W ant to build the most profitable relationship with your client? Try focusing on their profits first. When you focus on achieving client profitability, you create business relationships that are synergetic, whereby the whole is greater than the sum of its separate parts. A true partnership creates an equation where one-plus-one equals more than two. So, you have a choice to go it alone or partner with your clients.

Key to Partnering

How can we build the most effective partnerships with clients? Here are five keys to building the most effective partnerships with clients:

1. *Show your clients that you care about their success*, not just the most recent transaction. Successful partners never miss an opportunity to build the client's business, to help with the client's customers, and to solve the client's problems. Profit-focused professionals are more than order takers or transaction sellers. They have a completely different focus on the relationship. You will realize that the client's success will improve your success.

2. *Ask more than you tell.* Telling can put clients in a defensive posture quickly. Always be respectful of your client by guiding with good questions to ensure that you and the client are communicating before you give advice. Of course, the client wants your advice, but you will be more effective if you lead with questions. Implicit in the idea of asking is the concept of listening to what is said, not just hearing. You

want to listen to the words and the meaning. To get the meaning, you must listen with your eyes and your heart, because the meaning is transmitted from the emotion, not the words.

3. ***Clearly establish roles and goals.*** In successful partnerships, each partner fulfills his role with reliability. If it is possible to be misunderstood, you will be. Therefore, you must clarify who will do what by when. Put everything you can in writing so each party has a good record. And finally, make no promises you can't keep.

4. ***Be flexible.*** You have a standard approach to your practice, with standard systems and contracts. However, your partner may want one that is not cookie cutter. One of the keys to an effective partnership is to fashion a relationship that is, of itself, unique.

5. ***Communicate regularly and thoroughly.*** Call your client-partner regularly, not just when you need business. Call and visit on some periodic basis to communicate the nuances of the business partnership. If you only communicate around the business transaction, you will be relegated to vendor status. If you want to be a partner, communicate, communicate, and communicate.

Conclusion

When you focus on client profits, you both get the benefit of advisor status, plus you become more indispensable and obtain more repeat business. Remember, you must abide by state and federal rules and your code of professional conduct regarding independence.

88 Retreat and Advance 1

One of the best ways for you to become an insider with your clients is for you to help their top management focus on business strategy. Trends in leadership and management come and go, but the need for an executive team to get away, *visualize, strategize, prioritize, organize,* and *energize* is universal. You can be the catalyst for your best clients when you lead them in a strategic retreat.

Most of our clients have eliminated the term *retreat* for a more purposeful description like *go forward* or *advance.* The real purpose of an executive getaway is to focus the energy of a business on its mission. Every business executive team should hold such a meeting at least once a year. Here are some ideas to help you organize a client advance. For practice, you can run an advance for your own firm.

Visualize

Plan some time at the beginning of your meeting to review the vision and mission for you and your business. Two of our clients spend an entire weekend working on the mission of the individuals on the team as well as the mission of the business. Managers and employees can operate most productively within an organization that knows where it is going.

Too often, when a firm's mission is ill defined, the needs of key stakeholders are not being met. When the needs of clients, employees, families, and owners are not all addressed, serious problems undermine the success of your firm. Only when your mission is defined can you select the appropriate systems and strategies that will lead you to your vision.

Effective business planning is perhaps the single greatest challenge facing the small business owner today. Whether you call it a "retreat" or a "strategic planning session," going away from the business at least once per year to plan for the future is critical to a company's success.

With the fast-paced environment we operate in today, it is too easy to lose sight of the vision and the goal of balancing the business' goals with the objectives of the shareholders. Failure to plan is like starting the Boston Marathon with no idea where the finish line is.

Bob Reynolds,
Brady Wane & Schoenfeld,
Richmond, Indiana

Strategize

During one of our client's advances, the executive team examined their strategy for developing a technology consulting practice. The executive team members had a clear vision of the next three years: "to be the dominant financial advisory firm for small (less than $150 million in revenue) manufacturing businesses." The firm's mission is also clear: "to utilize our most-trusted-business-advisor role to help our clients succeed in a challenging world."

The technology strategy that had been used positioned the firm as a *vendor* of software. The executive team decided this strategy did not align with the vision of being an "advisory" firm and that being a vendor of someone's product threatened the perception of objectivity on which "the most trusted business advisor" role is founded. A more powerful, technology strategy emerged during the advance that is in alignment with the firm's vision and mission.

89 Retreat and Advance 2

The first time you hold an advance, you can spend all the time on developing a mission and vision. Once your vision and the process becomes established, you will spend more of your time on how to achieve specific goals.

Prioritize and Organize

With a solid mission in place, an executive team can select the action steps that are most important to the accomplishment of the firm's vision. Otherwise, everyone seems to let the latest "rush job" divert attention from the important actions.

Here's an example: A business had gotten behind on deliveries. Some customers were complaining and the employees were ducking calls because of the many complaints. One problem was leading to another. Once the timeliness problem was addressed at the advance, the executive team identified the bottlenecks and prioritized the steps to solving the problem. Within 30 days of the advance, systems for logging, preparing, reviewing, and streamlining delivery were revamped. Within 60 days all deliveries were timely. Had the problem not been prioritized, serious customer losses could have occurred.

Energize

There is something intangible that occurs when a team is focused on a common vision and mission. When the systems and strategies are in place to accomplish the vision, a powerful belief develops. Focus and belief can energize your clients' executive teams and your entire staff. The energy that surrounds an on-purpose staff will spark enormous results.

One of our clients has held strategic marketing advances for the past five years. Their 30% compound growth is a direct result of an executive team being on-purpose, being committed to the same goals, agreeing on systems and strategies, and holding each other accountable for results.

Conclusion

The process of firm planning sometimes doesn't look as practical as responding to immediate needs. However, when you run a good advance, it helps your clients avoid "fighting fires" and becomes very practical.

90 Leverage Up the Value Ladder

The value ladder is a way of looking at the value clients receive from our services. Services at the bottom of the ladder are commodities. Commodities are bought and sold by the pound, at the lowest possible price. You will have many competitors at the bottom of the ladder. As you begin to move up this imaginary ladder, client's price resistance will diminish.

The Top of the Ladder

Moving to the top of the ladder, clients view our services that have an impact on their organization with almost no price resistance. Operating at the top of the value ladder requires you to use leverage in your services delivery. In order to achieve leverage and climb the value ladder, here are some keys to help you be more successful:

1. *Select projects that will have a high degree of success.* For example, last year, in working with a partner group to jumpstart the firm's growth, we had a choice to work with two partners who needed a lot of intense help or two who were leaders. Since this was a newer client, I chose the two leaders because I knew their early success would encourage others that they too could succeed.

2. *Focus on working yourself out of a job.* When you focus your services on making your client self-sufficient, you empower their employees to perform the commodity-level work, while you focus at the top of the value ladder. You must work with your client to overcome the myth that only experts can do the job and you must help the client's personnel to be more effective with their time.

3. *Coach your clients to see the value of you working at the top of the value ladder.* Explaining the value ladder concept to your clients will help you communicate the power of this formula.

4. *Work personally with senior management and in groups with others.* Senior management has the most influence within the organization for advancing your services or project. Rather than work individually with lower-level personnel, you should structure group meetings and workshops to help them progress.

5. *Train others within the organization to do your job when you*

aren't present. We work with many marketing directors and coordinators to keep the momentum of our work progressing when we aren't present. These directors carry on our work after we are gone, and they are able to multiply the client's return on their consulting investment.

Conclusion

Working at the top of the value ladder is a good way to improve your client's profits *and* your profits from the services you provide. Moving up the ladder will require you to think and act differently.

91 Selling to the Top

Becoming an insider and selling to owners, board members, and top management takes a unique combination of *attitude* and *aptitude.*

Attitude

To operate successfully in the boardroom, you need the self-confidence to feel on equal footing with the top officers. Such an attitude also presumes that you can understand the issues facing the top officers. It means that you are willing to articulate your solutions in such a way that you can be a change agent in the business relationship.

Top officers exude power. If you are reticent about networking with top officers, you must push yourself to learn the ropes and overcome your fear. After you have met with a few chiefs (a common reference to CEOs, CFOs, CIOs, CAOs, and related titles), you will begin to relax as you realize they are just like you, but different. As my football coach used to say to get us to overcome our fear of the opposition, "he puts his pants on just like you."

Aptitude

Time is a precious commodity to top officers in businesses. The further up the food chain you move in a company, the more time sensitive your prospects and clients will be. For this reason, you will also need aptitude in dealing with the chiefs.

People who are unsuccessful selling to top officers waste time, don't tell the whole story, and communicate poorly.

Top officers and especially CEOs have learned to make decisions with very little information—they want only the key facts. Their jobs require them to make lots of decisions in a short amount of time. Many of them fear wasting time with someone trying to sell something. Investing her time wisely will enable a chief to make steady progress toward company objectives.

Before you meet with a top officer you must do your homework and know about the company and its problems. You should have other insiders on your side, if possible.

CEOs are particularly suspicious of a professional who only covers the upside and fails to cover the downside. In his book, *Think and Sell like a CEO,* Tony Parinello recommends you use a balanced reward equation to communicate your benefits. When you say that your service will save $400,000 in taxes, the CEO is thinking, "And how much audit risk or extra compliance costs will I have?" Be like Abraham Lincoln, who always gave both sides of the case in a debate to appear fair and to disarm potential counterarguments.

Last, communicating with CEOs takes skill. You must learn to cover the "bullet points" succinctly and accurately. As you cover the bullet points, use written materials to handle the details.

Conclusion

With the right attitude and aptitude, any professional can sell successfully to top managers, board members, and owners.

Strategic Directions

92 The One-Firm Concept = Brand

Building a brand can be a powerful force in your practice if your firm truly operates as *one* firm. Most firms operate as a collection of practitioners sharing overhead. Operating together as one firm enables you to create synergy when communicating with clients and prospects.

Synergy from One Firm

How can you tell if you are operating as one firm? Ask yourself a few questions:

- Is the partner compensation system built on the book of business mentality rather than each partner's total contribution to the firm?
- Does a significant amount of our revenue come from partners introducing other partners' services to clients?
- Do we have a system in place that will consistently achieve good service from partner to partner and from office to office?

Even beyond the desire to operate as—and present—a one-firm image, every professional firm needs to "reposition" themselves in the minds of the customer.

Using Branding

Branding can be the key to extending your most trusted advisor status to the new service areas you're offering. Do your clients think of you first when they need human resource services?

Business advice? If you haven't extended your brand in a way that redefines who you are, I guarantee you the answer is "no."

Branding is a method to build a larger—and possibly redefined—space in the minds of your customers. Successful branding connects what clients are passionate about buying with what you are passionate about delivering.

Branding is not just advertising or promotion. Your brand must permeate your entire operation. In order for your branding campaign to have impact, your marketing messages should express your firm's culture and values. Your messages should be clear and your operations should be consistent and congruous with the message.

Conclusion

Your brand may be an intangible asset, but never doubt that effective branding can deliver bottom-line results. Successful branding will enable your firm to obtain premium pricing, to receive more opportunities to serve clients and prospects, and to become recognized as a market leader.

93 Lead with Vision

Successful leaders have a vision for their business. Whether you are CEO of your firm or a practice leader, you will be more successful when you lead with vision.

The "Vision Thing"

What is a vision? A vision is reality in the future. A vision shows where you want to go and what things will be like when you get there. Vision is derived from the Latin word *videre,* which means "to see." Your vision can be a powerful driving force to keep your team members focused on the growth you want to achieve.

Working on your vision requires you to consider mission: What is it you want to do? Our mission is to transform the lives of professionals. We truly want professionals to be different after an encounter with us. For your mission to be powerful, it must make a difference. Without a difference, you will be just another vendor of services.

Usually, the difference you make with your clients will translate into competitive advantage for your firm. Prospects and clients use you because of the difference you make in their business.

Acting on Your Vision

Once your vision is in focus and linked to an appropriate mission, your strategy must support the achievement of your vision and mission. Remember, your strategy is more flexible than your vision or your mission. Your realized strategy may be quite different from your intended strategy, because you adapted along the way.

Once you have a clear vision, mission, and strategy, your attention must focus on getting the structure, systems, and staffing in alignment with your goals.

Structure and Systems

For example, if your vision calls for rapid and consistent growth, you must have structure, systems, and staffing that will support the growth. To achieve rapid growth, a firm must be able to make decisions quickly. We often encounter firms who have high growth strategies but because their structure is a partnership, the high growth cannot be achieved. A partnership structure, by its nature, is more deliberative and less concerned about making decisions quickly.

The same can be true with systems. For example, hourly billing and collection systems deter partner attention from serving the client. To achieve your vision, you must adopt systems that won't fight the achievement of your goals.

Conclusion

A team that is emotionally moved by their vision has the strength to overcome the obstacles of business life. A clear vision for your firm creates a good picture of your future. Sharing this picture with your associates can be a major motivator to them.

94 Strategic Alliances: The Whole Is Greater than the Sum of the Parts

by Kevin Poppen*

Has business life for your clients become more complex? How about competitive? Regulated? Are tax and legal issues more difficult? If your answer to any of these questions is in the affirmative, you believe as I do: "The demand for high-level professional services is growing, not declining." This phenomenon puts great pressure on the service professional who sees all the opportunities in the complexity, but does not have the capital to build the solution from the ground up.

Available Resources

A solution to this perplexing issue is to become involved in a strategic alliance with other similar professional service firms. One such alliance is the Enterprise Network. Enterprise Network is one of the largest alliances of professional service firms in the United States. Enterprise Network partners share resources and work together to strengthen the business skills of each partner.

What should you look for in strategic partners? The key ingredient I've found in successful alliances is that the cultures of each member must be synergistic. Each member must have a similar business philosophy and a need for each other's expertise and assistance. In addition, the most successful firms in an al-

---

*Kevin Poppen is President of Enterprise Network, LLC.

liance are those who have an inclination toward participation, enthusiasm for the mutual sharing of ideas and services, and a desire for sharing and open cooperation in alliance development.

Sharing the Benefits

Clearly, two or more heads are better than one. Partners always searching for a better answer for their clients tend to be the most successful.

Partners who believe in abundance are more apt to be open and cooperative. They want to share their best practices with the expectation that others will reciprocate. Everyone wins in this scenario. Professional firms that take the team approach to client service within their own firms only multiply those advantages when they participate in an alliance relationship.

Conclusion

If you want to serve your clients with better services, consider the benefits of a strategic alliance. These alliances offer you value, best practices, expertise, education, efficiency, productivity, and improved client relationships. Growing your firm through a strength-in-numbers approach can be powerful for you and your partners. An alliance with other service professionals will make the whole worth more than the sum of the parts.

95 Succeed by Failing More

You know the old story about the youngster who asked how to be successful. The successful professional said you need experience. And how do you get experience? You try and fail. The error of the past is the success of the future.

Encouraging Effort

How can you encourage your partners and professionals to fail more in marketing so they can succeed long-term? Can you create a forgiving or "brainstorming" attitude? In doing so, you will make your firm more dynamic.

A mistake is evidence that someone tried to do something. Nowhere is this truer than in selling accounting and legal services.

As professional firms are becoming more entrepreneurial and less bureaucratic, great managing partners and CEOs are encouraging experimentation and risk.

Business is too competitive to wait for perfection. In order to succeed in sales, you must risk failure time after time. All advertising, public relations, and direct mail programs have failure rates (nonresponse) that exceed 95%. But the 1% to 5% success can create excellent leads and pay for all your efforts.

Redefining Failure

Bill Jenkins, CEO of Kennedy & Coe, recently addressed his owner and management group with, "Setbacks are not to be considered failures. Instead consider breakdowns as breakthroughs, and disappointment as opportunity. This requires guts and self-confidence. Day after day, as a leader, you must re-assure people of the benefits of failure until everyone in our firm learns to embrace setbacks as windows to learning." I pre-dict Kennedy & Coe will succeed even more by learning from experimentation.

Networking can often seem fruitless. But the most powerful rainmakers have built a Rolodex of powerful people by sorting through the one-in-a-hundred odds at networking events.

Conclusion

In high-growth companies, failure is prized, not scorned as it is in many firms. In fact, almost all successful entrepreneurs have failed multiple times. This is how they learned how to succeed.

It's not *that* you fail, its *how you deal with the failure* that counts. Do you stop? Do you not try again? Only then do you fail.

If you are undaunted; if you learned from the failure; if you keep trying to obtain that impact client—then your "failures," mistakes, or experiments will ultimately lead to success.

TWENTY

Final Thoughts

96 Training for Results

Great advances have occurred in the professional training programs available today. Firms want a bigger payback from their investment in training. Accountants and attorneys are looking for courses that are satisfying, challenging, and rewarding. They want practical, exciting ideas for gaining efficiency and increasing their value to clients and prospects.

How to make training in technical areas work for you more generally will be addressed in the next strategy. Marketing and sales training has some obvious paybacks, starting with more business and the ability to select the kinds of clients you want for your firm.

Motorola and others repeatedly have shown that a dollar invested in training returns 15 to 30 times the investment. Yet many firms say, "I don't want to invest in training and then have people leave." But the more relevant question is, "Would you rather not invest in training and have your nontrained people stay?"

How to Make Training Work

Even the finest training will not succeed without three keys. The first key is top management's support. Top management must not only agree to the training, but they must also become strong adherents of developing new habits. To improve marketing and client relations, partners need to tell staff members, "We have been training you technically for years, but to advance further, let's work together to develop skills and habits that will hone your competitive edge."

The next important key is follow-up commitment by the firm and staff members to rise to the challenge of developing new habits. For example, we have added a self-directed 12-week follow-up program to many of our training courses. Firms need to hold follow-up marketing meetings, brown bag lunches, or periodic role-playing exercises to build new skills.

Third, commit yourself and your partners to train constantly in areas of client needs. Many professionals design their training classes around a good location or an interesting intellectual subject. These criteria should take a back seat to impact training.

Conclusion

The most successful professionals and firms are those that commit to excellence in training.

97 Use Continuing Education for Marketing

In many legal and accounting firms, CE, CLE, or CPE selling is a frequently neglected marketing tool. Continuing education (CE) is viewed as a burden rather than a beneficial sales tool.

Many professionals view their CE requirement with disdain. Some even cram their hours into the last month of the year and try to do as little as possible to maintain their licenses. I've even heard some complain to their clients about their CE requirements.

Every businessperson competing in today's economy knows that to stay ahead and on top of changes, their professional advisors must continuously upgrade their skills. The best and the brightest have adopted a lifelong learning attitude. Yet some professionals neglect their training and forego the tremendous marketing advantage it gives us.

Why not make a strong commitment to your training program and then use your efforts to market your practice? Whenever you plan to attend a training course of any type, consider how you might use the training to your marketing advantage. Here are a few examples.

Learn More Marketing and Selling Skills

In some states, such as California, attorneys can't take marketing CLE classes. However, even there, they can take customer service and ethics classes that deal with marketing issues. In most states, you can find classes that will improve your skills in this crucial area. You benefit your business, and receive CE credit besides.

Obtain Skills that Will Attract Clients

If your area of concentration is family businesses, why take a course in credit unions just because it is being held in Las Vegas? Clients of advisory firms are screaming for their professionals to add more value to the relationship by acquiring a deeper understanding of the clients' businesses. Don't be content with just a general understanding of your clients' businesses, limited by what they tell you. Become a decision influencer by learning how you can help your clients grow and prosper.

Let Your Clients Know about Your Commitment to Training

A while ago, I read a great article in *American Way* magazine, written by American Airlines' Chairman. The article was titled "Where School is Never Out" and covered American's commitment to training. Just reading the article made me feel safer about flying on American Airlines. My clients are now sending a similar letter to their clients. The letter emphasizes the value of their commitment to CE and how it can help the clients. This can only build their loyalty.

98 Coaching for Success

One of the crises many professional firms face today is a scarcity of loyal, talented, and experienced people. What if, when you were age 24, one of the partners of your firm, whom you respected, invited you for a cup of coffee. Then after some initial chitchat, the partner said to you, "I'd like to help you succeed in this business."

Develop Your Staff's Talents

What if that partner went on to say something like this: "We have several young staffers in our firm, but I'd like to coach you. We hired you because you are talented and I think you are outstanding. I want to help you succeed here or wherever your career takes you." And what if, over time, that partner followed through? He met with you, watched over you, guided you, and helped you make better choices and avoid mistakes.

Many of the best people gravitate to firms that recognize, pay for, and appreciate them. Yet too many firms use a sink-or-swim approach with their young talent and often the firm is the loser in the end.

There is a way to help cure this problem once and for all if it exists in your firm: Develop a formal coaching or mentoring program. A marketing coaching program can promote a can-do attitude throughout your staff. It can have a dramatic ripple effect throughout your firm. You can help your staffers build a business network. And, should your protégé leave your employ, you will have a friend for life.

How to Do It

Coaching for success can help both you and your employees develop dramatically better skills. For the most part, you should only coach one or two people at a time. Take them on sales calls, take them to Rotary Club, and take them home with you for a meal. Talk to your young associate about what it really takes to succeed. Pour out your wisdom and help them build relationships and grow.

A basic rule for coaching is to be friendly, frank, fair, and firm. With that formula, you can grow an excellent crop of future partners and build your firm for the long term. Coaching need only take an hour or so a week, but it should be consistent.

Want to learn more on how to coach? One of my favorite writers, Linda Richardson, has a book titled *Sales Coaching*. The book, published by McGraw-Hill, can be found in your local book store. Would you like to work more deeply and become a mentor? Whereas a coach is more skill focused, a mentor helps a protégé with his entire life: financial, physical, family, and faith. Bobb Biehl's Christian-based book titled *Mentoring* (Broadman & Holman Publishers) is an excellent choice for people of all faiths.

99 The Value of Training to Train

Give your staff the training to train. For example, students of our Rainmaker Academy are asked to teach what they learned at the Academy to other people at their offices. No matter what the content area, research shows that teaching enhances learning.

1. *People who are expected to teach pay more attention and learn more than students who do not expect to teach.* Preparing to teach will help embed the newly learned information more deeply into the attendees. *We highly recommend the material be taught within seven days of learning it.*

2. *Training gets passed on to managers and others in the firm who have not attended the training session.* Everyone who aspires

to leadership in professional firms must develop sales and marketing skills. Training just one person from a firm impacts only that person, whereas training three to five people is obviously more fruitful.

3. *Students subtly develop a mentoring and coaching program in selling skills.* One student should train three to five others in the firm. Training only a few others puts less pressure on the student and requires less logistical planning time. For ongoing training, teaching the same protégés over time creates strong relationships among the team members. If the teaching and coaching works well, the firm can expect to double the effects created from the student.

4. *Students develop leadership and teaching skills.* Good leaders model the activities for less experienced people to adopt. As students implement training and are held accountable for doing what they say they'll do, they become model leaders for their firm. When others are also held accountable, they develop significant credibility within the firm.

5. *Skills are delivered in a more cost-effective way.* When the participants teach the material they've learned to three other people, the per-person training cost to the firm drops considerably.

Summary

While the return on investment is still very powerful for one person's training participation, the return on investment becomes overwhelming using the training to train concepts.

100 Selling Is an Investment

One of the saddest events I witness in professional firms is the exodus of good people with experience. Yet this is just the group of people firms want to keep.

The policy of "up or out"—you make partner or you leave—strips firms of great experience. And it can cheat staffers who are not supported in doing what it takes to make partner. All too often, the staffers leave because they or their firms did not make a regular investment in their future. Partners who focus junior associates on the technical job at hand and then skimp on training and marketing may profit in the short run, but will lose long-term profitability.

Invest in Yourself

If you are an associate professional or staff member, avoid the easy trap of exclusive focus on your work. Make this the year that you invest in yourself (even if your firm does not). You will make yourself more valuable to the firm, and enjoy your job more as well.

Recently I asked a group of about 50 professionals if anyone had spent as much as $100 of their own money during the preceding 12 months on education. Two people raised their hands. Most people spend more on the outside of their heads (hair styles and cuts) than they do on the inside of their heads. At a recent marketing session, several of the people complained about the time (four hours) to read two paperback books on customer service. These 30-year-olds had begun the process of retirement at an early age.

Developing Your Selling Skills

Here are three key areas where you should invest in your marketing acumen now:

1. **Speaking and Writing**
    All professions are changing from technicians to communicators. Technology is becoming the "technician." Join Toastmasters International or take a speaking course. When you invest in your communication skills, you are creating a bright future for yourself. Write at least two articles for publication in the next year. If you do not feel qualified, ask someone who is an excellent writer to coach you and proof your material. Consider taking a creative writing course.

2. **Invest in Your Clients**
    Spend 2% to 5% of your time meeting with clients "off the clock." Find out about your clients' businesses. Learn about their problems, competition, and technology. Learn about their families, friends, and other acquaintances. Others are selling to your clients. Why shouldn't you? Don't assume you know what your clients want—ask them. Make certain you let your clients know you are investing in the relationships so they don't think you are billing them.

3. **Develop Two New Referral Sources**
    Your clients' other professionals and bankers are good places to begin developing referral contacts. If you will focus on developing two new strong referral sources a year until you've gained 12, you will never starve for new clients. Partners who have 12 acquaintances who send them just one referred lead a year are known as rainmakers. If you start building referral contacts early in your career, it is easy. If you wait until you've been in the business for 10

years, building 12 referral sources is hard. Inch by inch, anything is a cinch. Yard by yard, anything is hard.

101 Strategic Advances for Your Owner Group

A *retreat* is really a preparation to *advance* vigorously. That's why most of my clients now use the word *advance*. Holding an annual strategic advance will help you accomplish three key things:

- Strengthen your firm's overall strategy.
- Assure that your structure, systems, and staffing are in alignment with your strategy.
- Improve your commitment to action.

With a strategic advance, all of your owners can feel involved in the firm and its management processes, enthusiastic about marketing the firm to clients and others, motivated to achieve their individual objectives, and an important part of a committed team.

The principals of Waugh & Co. have conducted and facilitated advances for over 25 years. Our clients have used them with great success.

Management's Advance

While some advances are opportunities to "get away from it all," advances really should be for "getting into it." Educational and religious groups have used advances for years. But only recently have advances become popular for professional firms.

Objectives

We want to get away from the daily routine, the phone calls, the meetings, and all other activities that might distract us from the advance's objectives. A successful advance will have a major impact on the achievement of company goals. Therefore, it requires the unfettered participation of the attendees.

Leadership by top management in planning and conducting the advance is a must.

Advances can have any or all of several objectives. A group that hasn't worked together very long or closely can use the advance to build lines of communication and establish relationships among members. The advance should almost always be used to motivate the management team and build a spirit of teamwork. Achieving those objectives can be greatly enhanced by following a few simple rules:

- Keep the dress and atmosphere informal.
- Keep the size of the group manageable so everyone can and must participate.
- Arrange seating so participants are comfortable and feel part of the group.
- Eat meals as a group.
- Provide some social time for spontaneous interactions among members.
- Everyone remains at the advance from start to finish.

Conclusion

An advance offers an exceptional vehicle for educational programs for management. Remember, it's imperative that you know what your objectives are for the advance, or a substantial time and money investment will go down the drain.

Note: Appendix H contains an example of a pre-retreat questionnaire.

A

Sample Marketing Plan Items

Goals

- Firm-wide revenue goals
- Personal goals

Awareness Building Systems

- Advertising
- Trade journals
- Public relations
- Yellow Pages
- Articles published
- Sponsorships

Familiarity Systems

- Networking
- Speeches
- Memberships
- Seminars

Differentiation

- Niches
- Special services
- Uniqueness partnering
- Trade groups
- New services

Firm Perceptions

- Client service
- Dress code
- Attitudes
- Location, niches
- Office decor

Closing Sales

- Targeted prospects and referral sources listings

Client Marketing Systems

- Loyalty building
- Response time
- Referral development
- Newsletters
- Client satisfaction
- Meetings
- New services
- Seminars

Investment Budgeting

- Time
- Money

Services Mix

- Existing
- Niches
- New

Marketing Tools

- Brochures
- Materials
- Testimonials
- Trade shows
- Newsletters

- Advertising
- Seminars
- Radio
- TV

B

Checklist

Seminars, Workshops, and Training Programs

Seminars

- 30 minutes to 2 hours
- 2 or more attendees
- Presentation style is usually interactive
- Usually used for selling
- Free or paid admission

Workshops

- 1 to 4 hours
- 2 to 30 attendees
- Interactive style
- Selling is more subtle
- Usually paid admission, but could be free

Training Programs

- 1 to 8 hours
- Multiple days
- 2 or more trainees
- Used for relationship building—selling is very subtle
- Usually paid admission

C

Receptionist Training

Here is a 30-day training program for all the people who answer your phone.

1. **Rename your receptionist "Director of First Impressions."**
    Then, contact Career Track at 1-800-334-1018 for a low-cost video or audio seminar on telephone skills. Have all partners and people who answer the phones sit in on the training program.

2. **After the telephone training session, help your Director of First Impressions script responses to calls received by your office.**
    Make these responses a marketing opportunity every time.

3. **Provide your receptionist with all of the firm's marketing brochures and discuss them together.**
    Regularly review the services of the firm with your receptionist, and be sure that he or she knows the biographical info on each person in your firm.

4. **Ensure discretion with all callers on your whereabouts.**
    The receptionist should never say things like, "She isn't in yet" or "He's gone for the day." If you are unavailable, the caller should be given control of some options: talk to someone else, leave a message or voicemail, or send a fax or e-mail.

5. **Make every caller feel important by insisting on a warm, friendly voice from everyone who answers your phone.**

6. **Stop screening calls.**
   Last year, I asked an audience of 250 people how many were of-fended by call screening. Nearly 50% of the audience raised their hands. If 50% of your clients and prospects are offended by call screening, why would you do it?

7. **Assign your director of first impressions a prominent role on the marketing committee.**
   Find proactive marketing assignments.

8. **Most of all, make sure your director knows that the job is critical to the success of your marketing efforts.**
   Have him or her report to your firm's marketing director. Limit extra work and distractions.

   Remember, just one turned-off prospect can cost a
   full-year's marketing budget in lost revenue.

Lost Proposal Evaluation

How did you first know of _____ ?

Which firms proposed to do your work?

Which firm was successful?

Where would you rank _____ (our firm)?

What are your main needs for a law (or CPA) firm?

Who were the key decision influencers at your company?

Did your board or audit committee have input?

Did anyone outside your company have input? (like a lawyer or banker)

Did you contact any of our references?

How did their comments impact your decision not to engage us?

What were the three strongest points about our proposal?

What were the three major weaknesses?

What were the three strengths of the winner?

Did you have any reservations about the winner?

When making the final decision, what were the perceived risks you considered?

How much time did your personnel spend with each proposal team?

Did any of the decision influencers know people at the winning firm prior to the proposal process beginning?

Please rate whether you agree or disagree with the following:

1. _____ seems familiar with the problems related to my business.

2. _____ made me aware of the areas in which they could help me.

3. The _____ personnel seemed technically competent.

4. My staff and I were treated in a courteous and friendly manner.

5. _____ is a well-managed firm.

Do you have any other comments that would help us win future proposals?

Checklist

Client Business Review

- ☐ Call the CEO of the selected client and set a meeting time. Invite the CFO and other key executives of the business.
- ☐ Tell the CEO that there will be No Charge for your time—that you are making an investment in the relationship.
- ☐ Arrange for each person on your staff involved in the client work to participate in the meeting.
- ☐ Arrange for other key partners, such as your managing partner or concurring partner, to be present.
- ☐ Set the agenda so that the client personnel do 75% of the talking.
- ☐ You may want to feed them questions prior to the meeting that they can be prepared to answer at the meeting, such as:
  - Over the last three years, what has happened in your business that you are most proud of? What are you most disappointed with?
  - What are your major corporate goals over the next two to three years?
  - What key action steps do you plan to help you achieve your goals?
  - Do you anticipate any areas of difficulty in achieving your objectives?
  - How are you going to approach the areas of difficulty?
  - What do you see on the governmental front that may impact you?

☐ Ask each person how you can help him or her to be more successful in the performance of his or her job in the coming years.

☐ Maintain excellent notes and plan an internal follow-up session with your staff members to discuss ways you can help your client beyond the present assignments.

☐ Wrap up the meeting with a cordial luncheon or dinner. Make certain that each of your staff members is prepared to make conversation during the dining part of the meeting.

The Annual Referral Request Letter

(Your letterhead)

Date

Addressee

Dear Jon,

Please accept my sincere thanks for doing business with me. I look forward to a continuing and mutually profitable business relationship with you and your firm.

We are expanding our business in 200_ and I need your help. I am going to ask you for a small favor that will benefit us both.

Who do you know that has similar business needs to those I have helped you with or who may have needs described on the attached profile?

As a valued client of mine, you have learned that I view success as being solely the result of helping my clients prosper. With your help, I can expand my practice more efficiently than with costly mass-marketing approaches, and then I can invest the savings in serving you and other clients better.

Please take a moment to jot down a few names and phone numbers of people you feel would benefit from my service. Please fax or mail it back to me at your earliest opportunity. I will be sure to keep you informed of my progress.

Thank you for being my client and for helping me expand my practice.

With warmest regards,
(signed)

Staying in Contact with Specific Types of Referral Sources

Letters, phone calls, breakfast, lunch, dinner, and coffee work for all categories.

Clients

- Client seminars and reverse seminars
- Client business reviews
- Focus groups, client surveys
- Advisory boards

Attorneys

- Attorney newsletters
- CLE courses
- Mutual client meetings
- Office receptions

Bankers

- Banker newsletters
- Annual update sessions
- Boardroom meetings

CPAs

- Focus on practitioners who limit their practice

- Align with big national firms
- Establish local network for sole practitioners

Insurance Agents, Sureties, and Stockbrokers:

- Mutual seminars
- Send client newsletters

Real Estate Agents

- Sent client newsletters
- Annual continuing education

Example of a Pre-Retreat Questionnaire for Participants

Describe our firm as you would like others to view it.

_____

_____

What do you think is the firm's mission and purpose?

_____

_____

What new practice area should we consider?

_____

_____

Rank the importance of these areas, with 1 being the most important:

___ Obtaining prominent clients

___ Obtaining more clients

___ Working fewer hours

___ Making more money

___ Taking on more responsibility

___ Obtaining additional training

___ Expanding into other practice areas

___ Achieving a higher profile in the community

___ Improving client service

___ Improving staff morale

What should be the firm's number one goal for next year?

_____

_____

_____

What do you think will be your major contribution to the firm's success in the next year?

_____

_____

List the subjects you would like to see covered at our retreat.

_____

_____

_____

_____

Reference Guide

1. Introduction

Troy Waugh, *Power Up Your Profits: 31 Days to Better Selling*, Novato, CA: Select Press, 2000

David J. Lill, *Selling: The Profession*, DM Bass Publications, 2002

2. Prospecting

Rick Crandall, *Marketing Your Services: For People Who Hate to Sell*, New York: The McGraw-Hill Companies, 2002

Bill Good, *Prospecting Your Way to Sales Success*, New York: Scribner, 1997

3. Qualifiying

Bob Burg, *Endless Referrals: Network Your Everyday Contacts into Sales*, Updated Edition, New York: The McGraw-Hill Companies, 1998

Neil Rackham, *Rethinking the Sales Force: Redefining Selling to Create and Capture Customer Value*, New York: The McGraw-Hill Companies, 1998

4. Gaining Access to Decision Makers

Seth Godin, *Permission Marketing: Turning Strangers into Friends, and Friends into Customers*, New York: Simon & Schuster, 1999

Anthony Parinello and Denis Waitley, *Selling to VITO: The Very Important Top Officer*, Avon, MA: Adams Media Corp, 1999

5. Identifying Decision Influencers

Stephen E. Heinman and Diane Sanchez, *The New Strategic Selling*, New York: Warner Books, 1998

Dick Connor, and Jeff Davidson, *Getting New Clients*, Second Edition, Hoboken, NJ: John Wiley & Sons, 1992

6. Discovering Problems

Linda Richardson, *Stop Telling, Start Selling: How to Use Customer-Focused Dialogue to Close Sales*, New York: The McGraw-Hill Companies, 1997

Charles D. Brennan, Jr., *Sales Questions That Close the Sale: How to Uncover Your Customers' Real Needs*, New York: AMACOM, 1994

7. Developing Needs

Neil Rackham, *SPIN Selling*, New York: The McGraw-Hill Companies, 1988

Stephen E. Heiman and Diane Sanchez, *The New Conceptual Selling*, New York: Warner Books, 1999

8. The "R" Word

Robert B. Cialdini, *Influence: The Psychology of Persuasion*, Revised Edition, Richmond, BC: Quill, 1998

Rick Crandall and Aldonna Ambler, *Celebrate Selling the Consultative Relationship Way*, Corte Madera, CA: Select Press, 1998

9. Building Like and Trust

Steven R.Covey, *Seven Habits of Highly Effective People*, New York: Simon & Schuster, 1990

Robert Bruce Shaw, *Trust in the Balance: Building Successful Organizations on Results, Integrity and Concern*, San Francisco: Jossey-Bass, 1997

10. Demonstrating Capabilities

Michael Treacy and Fred Wiersma, *The Discipline of Market Leaders: Choose Your Customers, Narrow Your Focus, Dominate Your Market*, Cambridge, MA: Perseus Publishing, 1997

Spring Asher and Wicke Chambers, *Wooing & Winning Business*, Hoboken, NJ: John Wiley & Sons, 1997

11. Handling Objections

Al Ries and Jack Trout, *Marketing Warfare*, New York: The McGraw-Hill Companies, 1997

Tom Reilly, *Crush Price Objections*, Motivation Press, 1999

12. Persuading Decision Influencers

Bob Kantin, *Strategic Proposals: Winning the Big Deal*, New York: Vantage Press, 1999

Harry Beckwith, *Selling the Invisible: A Field Guide to Modern Marketing*, New York: Warner, 1997

13. Minimizing Risk

Scott West and Mitch Anthony, *Story Selling for Financial Advisors: How Top Producers Sell*, Chicago, IL: Dearborn, 2000

Lynda C. Falkenstein, *Nichecraft: The Art of Being Special*, Second Edition, Niche Press, 1993

14. Great Service Builds Loyalty

Hal Rosenbluth, and Diane McFerring Peters, *The Customer Comes Second: Put Your People First and Watch 'Em Kick Butt*, New York: HarperBusiness, 2002

Michael LeBouef, *How to Win Customers and Keep Them for Life: An Action-Ready Blueprint for Achieving the Winner's Edge*, New York: Simon & Schuster, 1997

15. Building Profits

Ron Baker, *The 2001 Professional's Guide to Value Pricing*, San Diego, CA: Harcourt, 2001

Mack Hannan, *Consultative Selling: The Hannan Formula for High-Margin Sales at High Levels*, Seventh Edition, New York, AMACOM, 2003

16. Offering Dessert

Martha Rogers and Don Peppers, *The One to One Future*, Redfern, Australia: Currency, 1996

Neil Rackham, *Major Account Strategy*, New York: The McGraw-Hill Companies, 1989

17. Soliciting Referrals

Robert Davis and Ivan R. Misner, *Business By Referral: Sure Fire Way to Generate New Business*, Bard Press, 1998

Thomas J. Stanley, *Marketing to the Affluent*, Reprint Edition, New York: The McGraw-Hill Companies, 1997

18. Becoming an Insider

Tuleja Miller and Stephen E. Heiman, *Successful Large Account Management*, New York: Warner, 1992

Larry Wilson, *Stop Selling, Start Partnering: The New Thinking About Finding and Keeping Customers*, Hoboken, NJ: John Wiley & Sons, 1996

19. Strategic Directions

David H. Maister, *Managing the Professional Services Firm*, Detroit, MI: Free Press, 1997

Al Ries and Jack Trout, *Bottom-Up Marketing*, New York: Plume, 1990

20. Final Thoughts

Jim Collins, *Good to Great: Why Some Companies Make the Leap . . . and Others Don't*, New York: HarperCollins, 2001

Al Friesw, *Focus: The Future of Your Company Depends on It,* New York: HarperBusiness, 1997

Index

Troy has it right. Marketing is a process, not an event! My experience clearly validates his statement that "business people conduct business with people they like and trust'. There are many processes that work, however, the most successful rainmakers are the people who have a process and the discipline to follow it.

David Morgan, Co-Managing Partner
LBMC Financial
Nashville, TN

Troy Waugh combines the power of experience and knowledge to provide the dedicated professional with a successful way to offer services. As important, Troy provides diagnostic tools to help determine why on-going efforts may not be successful and to turn those failures into learning experiences. Make no mistake, Troy is about action and success, not just more knowledge about professional sales and marketing. The book is an easy read, with short, to the point, easily absorbed chapters. This book will be a must read for anyone who strives for success in selling professional services.

Kevin J. Moser CPA, CVA, President
Anneken & Moser, PSC
Edgewood, KY

It was a pleasure to read Troy's new book. It is an easy and logical read with many good ideas. I have used some of the ideas already and intend to implement many of the others. Great Book!

Joseph Brown, CPA, Managing Partner
MelhiserEndresTucker
New Albany, IN

The principles found in Troy's book are powerful and everlasting. Those principles are analogous to those in farming. Farmer prepares the ground, sows the seed, cultivates the sprouts, allows the crops to grow for a season, harvests the crops and goes to market. Cycle is repeated every year. I see the marketing investment as a cycle whereby seeds are constantly being sown and harvests are constantly being reaped. The farmer should plan to use only the good ground and likewise the marketing professional should evaluate at all times their target market. I appreciate how Troy has put these concepts into a detailed yet easy to use format.

Chris Griffin, Blankenship CPA Group, PLLC
109 Westpark Dr. Ste. 430, Brentwood, TN

After 33 years of public accounting experience with Ernst & Young (23 years) and Coulter & Justus, PC (10 years), I could probably write my own book when it comes to marketing professional services. After reading 101 Marketing Strategies, I realize Troy has a multitude of great ideas that are so practical, you say "Why didn't I think of that?

Sam Coulter, Managing Partner
Coulter & Justus
Knoxville, TN

It's another Sunday afternoon and I'm trying to outsmart my weekly planner. Monster Monday and the five weekend phone messages are guaranteed to knock me off my schedule, no matter what! Early afternoon Monday, just when I am ready to throw in the towel on my agenda, Troy Waugh's new book talks clearly to me: "If you cannot sell, you are prone to take only the work assigned to you or the prospects who call you because no one else wanted them.

Edward F. Moran, Jr.
MBA, CPA-AZ/CA, ABV, CVA
Moran, Quick & Associates, P.L.L.C.
6417 E. Grant Road, Tucson, AZ 85715

101 Marketing Strategies demystifies the selling process. Aptly named, this book delivers a blueprint for the professional who also sells. In simple, straightforward language, Troy Waugh conveys a wealth of information that anyone who owns a service-related business would be foolish to be without. I found the dialogue questions particularly helpful, along with the section on uncovering prospect problems. I will use this book each time I review and update my sales and marketing strategies.

William Lohrey
Lohrey & Associates, P.L.L.C.
Tulsa, OK

Troy's new book is an ideal quick read for our newer associates. The tools and guidelines are spelled out, so the newer associate will have no excuse. Excellent book.

Fred A. Lockwood
Fred Lockwood & Associates
Scottsbluff, NE

Troy's new book, just like The Rainmaker Academy, is a common sense approach to getting business, if you have the common sense to read the materials and follow the advice.

Phil Salvador
Mulcahy, Pauritsch, Salvador & Co
Orland Park, IL